Present and Accounted For

by

Tom Oestreicher

Corps Badge

Army of the Potomac
2nd Corps
2nd Division
3rd Brigade
14th Indiana Volunteer Infantry

authorHOUSE™

1663 Liberty Drive, Suite 200
Bloomington, Indiana 47403
(800) 839-8640
www.AuthorHouse.com

First published by AuthorHouse 11/15/04

ISBN: 1-4184-8992-1 (sc)

Library of Congress Control Number: 2004095879

Printed in the United States of America
Bloomington, Indiana

This book is printed on acid-free paper.

Copy Editor: Marcia Wilson
Advantage Editorial Services
Sycamore, Illinois

Cover photo and design by Kelly Marks

Dedication

To my wife, Marilyn:
My greatest fan and soul mate
and
to the memory of
the thousands of
Civil War dead who
remain unaccounted for

Acknowledgements

My son, Chris, and my daughter, Deanna, for their support.

My grandchildren, Samantha, McKinzie, Charlie, and Jeffrey for being the joy in life that they bring. My many students who helped with their computer expertise. My many friends and extended family who offered their encouragement.

Chapter 1

*"Accept the challenges, so that you may feel the
exhilaration of victory."*

Gen. George S. Patton

The muffled drumbeats echoed off the rolling hills surrounding
the cemetery. It was as if every soul buried at Arlington was
coming alive to witness this historic moment. The crowd of
onlookers was numbered far beyond anyone's expectations;
tens of thousands, perhaps half a million.

What a curiosity this is...

Washington hadn't seen anything like this since President
Kennedy's funeral in November 1963. I remember that day
as if it was yesterday. Who could forget? Every American
alive at that time remembers exactly where they were when
they heard the news of J.F.K.'s assassination. Now here we
are were hearing those drums thirty years later.

The caisson slowly entered through the grand iron gates of
Arlington National Cemetery. The stone-faced honor guards
from nearby Ft. Meyers sat atop the caisson in perfect posture.
This duty was perhaps the grandest of their young military
careers. The color guard preceded the caisson. A thirty-three
star American flag was carried in honor of this special veteran.
The grand old flag took the wind and was in full array. The

Indiana state flag was to the left and slightly tilted, bowing to the national symbol. The six black-draped white stallions slowly edged the caisson deeper into the cemetery.

Behind the caisson marched 3,500 Civil War reenactors dressed in much too authentic-looking uniforms. They came from virtually every state to take part in this, their finest moment. What an honor to be here . . .

The procession moved slowly forward under a flawlessly beautiful blue sky. I can see all sorts of dignitaries. Governors from once Confederate states, Governors of Union states, famous historians, and right in the middle of them all, the vice president. I never dreamed that my little research would end like this. What have I done? Somehow this single event seems to bind us all together again.

The commanders of the army, the navy, and the marines represented every branch of the military that was active during the Civil War. There must be at least a dozen Civil War–vintage caissons and artillery pieces in the procession. The red-trimmed artillery uniforms are strikingly beautiful. What meticulous care has given to these historic pieces. The procession just keeps coming.

My wife, Marilyn, tugs on my sleeve signaling that it is time to take our place, at the burial site. The family members have already been seated alongside the oak casket. The pallbearers, all from Ft. Meyers, stand at attention beyond the crowd. Seating for five hundred has been arranged. Lined up my right are the artillery pieces and seven blue uniformed soldiers. I assume they are the rifle squad and will fire the seventeen-gun salute, which is normally reserved for generals and admirals. The whole affair seems perfect.

The pastor of St. John's Lutheran Church stepped forward. Pastor Brigham is a tall man of about forty years old. The family selected him to deliver a simple, but faithful graveside sermon. Of course the pastor never knew the deceased, none of us had.

Chris Brigham has been a pastor for about eleven years. He knows there is something very special about this particular funeral. It is his first where he didn't know the family or the deceased. He must be thinking, *How in the world do I eulogize this person? What can I, or anyone who didn't know him for what he was in life say that is meaningful?*

Chris looked directly at me for what seemed to be nearly a minute before he said anything. He knows that I am the one responsible for this whole affair, and I am the one who brought him here. Finally, in a deep, clear voice that denotes his authority, he asks that we bow our heads in prayer.

The crowd is silent and the world itself appears to stand still. The soul of a long forgotten soldier is about to be formally handed back to its Creator.

My solace is interrupted by a young boy standing in front of me. He appears to be about eight years old. He reaches up and pulls on my necktie. Our eyes meet. I know he is a relative of the deceased, but I have forgotten his name, even though I met the family at a reception last week. His mother, the great-great-granddaughter of the deceased, is seated directly in front of him. This little guy looks up at me and in a whisper asks, "How did you find my great-great-great-grandfather?"

I focus on his nametag. All family members were provided nametags by the military. In large bold print is his name, John Jacob Gates. Under his name in slightly smaller print are the words, Great-Great-Great-Grandson. For a moment I hear Pastor Brigham say something about service to country and honor.

As I glance at young John looking up at me in the middle of this prayer, I wonder what to say. Words don't come. I begin to think back over the past two years, recalling all the research and work it took to accomplish this task.

If I remember correctly, it all started on a crisp October day in northern Illinois. It was one of those days when the sky was crystal clear and the air seemed purer than normal. In that part of the country people relish each of these days before the snows fly.

I had been waiting for my friend Wes to meet me. Wes has been one of my closest friends for many years. I would guess probably twenty years at least. We are both Civil War buffs. We have shared many hours discussing aspects of battles, magazine articles, movies, virtually everything related to the Civil War. Our wives thought we were nuts to spend so much time and energy on something over and done with.

Wes wanted to meet me to discuss something he had read that might be of real interest to me as a researcher. Wes Wilson was always reading, usually about woodcarving or woodworking projects. I couldn't imagine what he had come across that would require such urgent interest.

At any rate, I was early for our meeting and enjoying a badly needed cup of coffee. I never need a reason to have coffee; any occasion is fine with me. My research is not very exciting sometimes. I often have to force myself to stick with it and see it through. The university provides me with a computer and a cubicle to call home, but a coffee shop like this would do me just fine.

My waitress had refilled my coffee three or four times. I was just about to give up meeting Wes when I saw him coming across the parking lot. Oh well, let's have some more coffee!

Wes was excited that day. He was late because he had misplaced the all-important article. Wes couldn't wait to see my reaction. He pushed it in front of me even before he sat completely down in the booth. "Take a look at this," he said.

I caught the title and looked at Wes. "This is it?" I couldn't believe that I had sat here for nearly an hour to see an article about an Indiana Civil War regiment that had several of its members unaccounted for. No big deal for a Civil War unit. Hell, 70 percent of the soldiers killed in the Civil War are unidentified. Wes said, in an almost demanding tone, "Read it."

The title was "Missing Hoosiers: Our Forgotten Warriors." I must have seen dozens of articles like this over the past twenty years. What could be so different about this one?

The author was Gabe Warren, a grad assistant at Oglethorpe Christian College in Sussex, Indiana. I found the article interesting, but certainly nothing out of the ordinary. Wes leaned across the booth and pointed out a name on the list of missing infantrymen. I pulled a pen from my shirt pocket and circled the name of Private Thomas Overland. Wes said, "Mary and I think this Overland guy might be a relative. We know that her family lived in the southeastern Indiana area before the war."

Looking at me over the brim of his coffee cup, Wes said, "Mary and I thought you would enjoy doing the research." *Isn't this great?* I remember thinking. *Just what I need, another project. Like the stack on my desk at work isn't enough for me to do!*

After reading the complete text of the article, some things became a little clearer. Gabe Warren was working on his Ph.D. in history. His dissertation was on Indiana Pensions for Civil War Veterans. According to the article, Warren had identified twenty-three soldiers from the 14th Indiana Volunteer Infantry with incomplete service records. From my experience as a researcher I know that incomplete records usually mean they were killed in action and never reported or were missing and never reported. The soldiers listed were:

Robert Ackley	Private	Co. D
Ben Alt	Corporal	Co. K
James Bannon	Corporal	Co. F
Thomas Bean	Private	Co. A
Jacob Bendalone	Sergeant	Co. I
William Bergman	Corporal	Co. H
James Blocker	Sergeant	Co. C
Thomas Caldwell	Private	Co. I

Charles Carr	Corporal	Co. C
Elijah Childers	Private	Co. G
Charles Dix	Private	Co. A
Asher Davidson	Private	Co. D
Edgar Franklin	Private	Co. E
Frederick Gale	Private	Co. K
Daniel Hales	Private	Co. I
David Hayes	Corporal	Co. B
Norman Kinder	Private	Co. A
Hiram Oats	Private	Co. C
Thomas Overland	Private	Co. I
Micah Pandarri	Private	Co. B
Horace Tidall	Sergeant	Co. A
Jacob Winslow	Private	Co. G
William Wollman	Private	Co. K

Apparently Mr. Warren had mustering-in records for these twenty-three men, but nothing more. *Mustering* was a military term used similar to what we would refer to as registering or enlisting today. When a soldier was discharged, he was said to be "mustered" out of the service. Records for Civil War units are usually very accurate. The military back then was completely different than it is today.

Regiments were organized from the various counties within each state. Some regiments were even organized within factories or firehouses for that matter. A regiment was made up of about one thousand men. They were divided into ten companies of about one hundred men each. That was the plan anyway. Depending on the population of any given county, regiments were sent to war with whatever numbers they had available! According to Warren, the 14th Indiana was formed in Terre Haute in May 1861 for one year's service. It may have been formed from a combination of counties, too. It would be hard to tell without reviewing all the mustering records firsthand.

Wes was waiting for an answer. I thought for a moment. Of course I knew I'd do the research. Marilyn would understand. She says I never say no to anything, especially something to do with history! "Wes," I said, "I'd be glad to do this for you and Mary. It sounds like a lot of fun. I haven't done Civil War research for some time, and it'll be a nice break from the routine at the university." I was committed. Wes smiled a smile that said, "I knew you'd do it."

Back at work, things were crazy. The joys of a researcher! I was doing a massive project for Dr. Darling in the anthropology department. Joanne Darling was always doing something related to female primates and baboon social development. I don't know; I just do the research! I thought this would tie me up for some time. I was right. What I thought would be a couple of weeks turned into months.

Every once in a while I would catch myself taking a glance at the article sitting on top of a stack of papers on my credenza. In my line of work, there are always piles! I'd make time to get to it someday. Someday.

The winter of 1987 was a real bear, cold beyond belief. The good thing was that work was fairly slow. It was a nice break from our research department's usual pace. Requests for research from the university faculty were way down. I finally had some free time. I admit it took me awhile, but I managed to find that article. It had become buried in a pile, almost destined for membership in the "eternally lost papers club"! After all, it had been nearly five months since Wes introduced me to it. I thought I had better read it again to clear the cobwebs from my memory.

Over the next few weeks I spent a little time here and there between projects at work organizing how to go about researching Civil War records. It had been a long time since I did anything like this. It would be a challenge! Finally I decided to stop reinventing the wheel and planned to call Gabe Warren. He had already done the basic research. It sounded like a logical place to start.

I didn't know how big or small Oglethorpe College was but I did manage to get their phone number from directory assistance. I made the call. "Oglethorpe Christian College, Emily speaking. Where may I direct your call?" I asked for Gabe Warren's extension. Emily asked me, "What department is that in, sir?"

Of course I had no idea, so I guessed. "Research department, no, try the history department."

"Please hold, sir, I'll transfer your call."

The phone rang for what seemed forever. Finally a young female with a very mellow voice answered, "History, Dr. Warren's office." Well, I got the right place on my first try, off to a good start, or so it seemed. I introduced myself and said that I was doing some research on my own that may be of interest to Dr. Warren.

In the background I could hear someone ask, "Who is it, Samantha?" The young lady explained that it was someone who wanted him to do some research. Oh boy! That is about the last thing any researcher wants to hear. Reluctantly, Gabe Warren took the phone and asked in a rather disturbed tone, "Who is this?"

I began by telling him I was Michael Carls from Moss University in Illinois. He didn't seem overly impressed! I came right to the point. "I read your article on Hoosier Warriors. I have a friend who thinks he may be related to one of your missing soldiers." Again, silence on the other end.

"Well," said Gabe, "I don't have any additional information on any of those listed in the article. I don't think I can help you."

Fearing that he would hang up, I hurriedly interjected, "That's okay, I want to help you locate as many of these guys as possible. I have some really high-tech links that should help us." Again, silence!

"I don't know if I'll have the time. I moved on from that topic once I completed my doctorate." There was a pause. "I suppose it wouldn't hurt to give it some kind of a try. I have no idea where to start. I used everything I could find just to get that list alone! What do you suggest?"

"I have a couple of days off coming to me. Why don't I come to Sussex and we can plan things from there?" Gabe didn't respond right away. I could hear him turning pages in the background, probably checking his calendar.

"Mike . . . is it okay to call you Mike? I can meet you on Thursday, the 17th. Is that okay with you?"

I shrugged my shoulders at the phone and said, "Sure."

Marilyn came home from work at 5:00. I was waiting in the kitchen. "Marilyn, I have a great idea for the two of us. How would you like to get away for a couple of days and do a road trip?"

"Where?" asked Marilyn suspiciously.

"Well, honey, I was thinking of beautiful southern Indiana. How does that sound?"

With her head tilted, she smirked, "And why would I want to go to southern Indiana?"

"Well, there is this college there and I need to meet someone to discuss an article Wes has shown me. You remember, the one about the missing Civil War soldiers? You do remember, don't you?"

"You want me to miss work so you can hunt for some missing soldiers?"

"I thought you might enjoy getting away for a couple of days. You know, motel, pool, relaxing!"

"Tell you what, I can't make plans for a replacement at work that quick. We're already on a tight schedule. Why don't you take the trip and enjoy a couple of days. You love digging into old records and diaries. I'd just be in the way. Have a great time!"

"You wouldn't mind if I went alone?"

"Have at it, Mikey. I think I can manage on my own!"

For the next couple of days all I could think about was how to go about researching Civil War records. I finished up the two projects I had been working on for Dr. Darling. She would be pleased! Of course I knew that there would be more waiting for me when I got back. Joanne never ran out of things for me to do. I heard she had a never-ending honey-do list of things to keep her husband, Douglas, busy at home. She is one organized lady!

Having a lot of shelves in my cubicle was an occupational mistake. You give me a place to stack papers and I'll take advantage of it. At least I thought my piles were organized! I tried to clean up as much as possible before my trip. Young Deanna Hovland was going to fill in for me while I was gone to Sussex. She really only needed to answer the phone. She could hardly screw up that!

Deanna was usually a pretty quiet person; however, she liked listening to rock music while reading or working on the computer. I was just the opposite, quiet please! I guess my office mates found me fairly boring that way. I knew Deanna would mind the store in my absence.

I spent Monday and Tuesday wrapping things up. Deanna knew the routine well enough that I didn't need to spend much time with her. If nothing else, Joanne Darling would find something for her to do!

Leaving work at noon was a great idea. I was looking forward to a relaxing afternoon drive. I was so anxious to get out of the office that I almost completely forgot about my meeting with Wes at the university library. Wes and I were meeting on campus to go over some final questions and information that he had about Mary's family. I found the last parking place in the farthest corner of the library parking lot. It was a nice hike.

The Charles C. Smith Library was a massive, old, redbrick building. To freshman students it was the campus monster: dark, dingy, with hard oak tables and chairs. It reeked uncomfortable. It just looked like something out of an old movie. I think if you sneezed it would echo for an hour.

Wes was waiting at a table in the center of the main floor. A green bankers light was casting a dim glow. I recognized his coat and bushy hair. No mistake about it, it was Wes. As I sat down across from him, He handed me an old white envelope.

"Okay Wes, let's see what you've got here." I said.

"Mary has had this in her cedar chest for the past twenty years. Her mother gave it to us."

I opened the envelope and unfolded a brown tri-fold document. On the cover it said *Wm. Dover, Pension Agent, New York.* I had seen several of these over the years. The federal government had contracted with private accounting firms after the Civil War to handle payments for pensions and other retirement plans. The name Wm. Dover was known by virtually every Civil War researcher. The sheer numbers of soldiers that came from the New England area was astounding. Everything looked authentic. Penciled on the inside was the name *Thomas Overland/1896, July 2.* Judging from past experience that usually meant the date a veteran died and the end of pension benefits. The boxes to the right side of the document were labeled *Spouse* and *Widow*. In this case, the Widow box was checked. It wasn't a lot, but it is a start. Gabe Warren should see this material. It won't tell him much about one of his missing infantryman, but at least he'll know that he wasn't killed in battle.

I looked up from the paper and told Wes, "This is a good start. See if Mary can find anything else in the family Bible, or maybe a diary."

Wes reached into his coat pocket and handed me a gold pocket watch. It was worse for wear, but a family treasure for sure. "Here," he said. "Open it up and read the inscription."

I took the watch and gently pried the back open. The inscription was worn, but legible.

Pvt. Thomas Overland, Co. I, 14th Indiana
Service with honor
Gov. Conrad Baker
Dec. 17, 1871

"Wes, do you have any idea why he was given the watch on December 17? And why in 1871?"

"Mike, we have no idea at all. We just remembered seeing that watch at Mary's mother's house years ago."

"I'll run it by Dr. Warren. Maybe he can tie it to a regimental reunion or something on that date."

"It's probably nothing special, but it would be nice to find out what it means."

Wes stared at me across the table for a few lonely seconds and said in a most sincere voice, "I wish I could go with you on this trip."

Through the dim light of the bankers lamp, I could see how serious he was. Wes and I had shared hundreds of discussions on the Civil War. Here I was about to embark on a journey to do some real historical research on a subject we both loved dearly. I never thought of asking Wes to come with me. It was too late now, my bags were packed and the car was ready to roll: perhaps next time. There will be a next time, won't there?

"Wes, let me see where this little expedition takes me. If I need to go back to Oglethorpe, let's plan a few days together." I had no idea if I would ever be going to Oglethorpe again.

We said our good-byes and I headed home to spend an hour or so with Marilyn before hitting the road.

Marilyn was home on her lunch hour. Usually she stayed in her office at the bank and had a sandwich and an apple. She planned on seeing me off today and was in the kitchen where she had made me some fresh cookies for my trip. What a wife, always thinking of my manly figure!

"What is that I smell?" I said, as I walked into the kitchen.

"Oh, nothing. Just a little treat for me while you're gone."
I knew better. "You never eat more than a couple of your grandmother's chocolate cookies. I just might have to help you with the rest." Somehow those cookies made it into a bag and into my car at the same time. Amazing!

After a short time putzin' around the house and double-checking my clothes and such, it was time to get going. I kissed Marilyn good-bye and walked to the car. Marilyn stood on the back porch, extended her arm, and gave me a final wave. "Be careful and call when you get there." I nodded and blew her a kiss from across the yard.

I had a good 400-mile drive in front of me. If all went well, I could be in Sussex by 8:00. The weather was good and all systems were go.

The first 150 miles had to be the longest I have ever driven. Anyone familiar with Route 47 heading toward Champaign, Illinois, knows what I am talking about. Nice little towns, but boring. The scenery in central Illinois is not the stuff you see on postcards. I guess the word *flat* was invented here!

As I traveled into Indianapolis I caught myself struggling to find the correct exit. Traffic was congested for a Wednesday afternoon. What I forgot was that it wasn't 4:30 anymore, it was 5:30 here–something to do with Indiana having two time zones.

Great, I lost an hour!

I stopped at a fairly nice-looking restaurant just off the Interstate 65 South exit. I guess losing an hour makes one feel like it's suppertime. Right away I noticed how the people seemed friendlier than those up north. My waitress was young, probably a high school student, with a pleasant smile and big brown eyes. My meal wasn't memorable, but good just the same. It was 6:25 and I headed for my car to get back on the road. I knew it was getting late and I still had a good drive in front of me.

At a rest area thirty miles south of Indianapolis I gazed at a wall map in the lobby. I pinpointed Sussex and guestimated how long it was going to take me to get there. I thought it best to find a motel and call it quits for the day. I only had so much time to do this.

The Mayflower Motel was just off the Interstate. Nothing fancy, a well-needed bed, a phone, color T.V., and heat. The $21.95 a night wasn't going to break me, but it was an unplanned expense. I asked the desk clerk about Sussex and he gave me some advice on taking a shortcut. I wanted to make up the time lost, but I always hesitate with "shortcuts." At any rate, I planned on getting up early, having my free continental breakfast of rolls and coffee and heading out. I knew I'd be in Sussex and at Oglethorpe College at about 10:00. I called Marilyn to let her know where I was.

The phone rang twice and a very sleepy voice answered. "Hello."

"Hi honey, its me. I didn't want you to worry. I didn't make it to Sussex, I forgot about the Indiana time change. I stopped south of Indianapolis and had supper. How was your day?"

Marilyn paused and said, "Oh, it was okay. I just came home after work and did the usual around the house and then watched T.V. How was your drive?"

"It's going fine. I just underestimated the distance. I 'm at a motel off of 65. I'll get up early and head out. I should be in

Sussex midmorning. I just wanted to give you a call before it gets any later."

"Well," said Marilyn, "that's good. I think I'll just go to bed. You sleep well and call me tomorrow night, okay? And good luck with Dr. what's-his-name!"

"Okay, hun, have a good night. Call you tomorrow. I love you."

♣

Chapter 2

*"You can make more friends in two months by becoming
interested in other people than you can in two years by
trying to get other people interested in you."*

Dale Carnegie

My travel alarm woke me from a deep sleep. That had to have
been one of the best night's rest I ever had in a motel. I was
much more tired than I thought. I remember thinking, *How
much farther is Sussex?*

I opened my official state map of Indiana. I guess the nearest
town to the motel was Franklin. Well, let's see. According to
my thinking, if I took the Interstate about twenty-two miles to
Columbus and hopped on State Route 7 that should take me
pretty close, maybe into North Vernon. That's about forty-five
miles from here. From there I'd guess it to be another twenty-
five miles, max, to Sussex. Total should be around seventy-
five or eighty miles. A little over an hour drive, no sweat!

The drive on Route 7 was no picnic—two lanes, narrow, and
in need of repair. Once into North Vernon I picked up Route
50 east through several small towns—Nebraska, Holton,
and finally, Versailles. The short drive south of Versailles to
Route 129 was quick. At Cross Plains I stopped for gas and
asked for final directions to Oglethorpe College. I was only
two miles away.

Once I left Cross Plains, I immediately entered Switzerland County. Interesting name. I'd have to research that someday.

Ahead of me on the right was a sign that read:

Sussex
Pop. 4000

Here at last!

As I drove through the business district, it was like taking a step back in time. The sidewalks were raised, providing a curb for parking. It was an old town. The storefronts were dated near the rooftops, 1848, 1860, and 1871.

The Ben Franklin Store was the largest store in town. Marilyn's Café was next door. *I'll have to tell Marilyn about this when I get home*, I thought. Little did I know then that I would be spending many hours here drinking countless cups of coffee.

I found out later that the town had been settled in 1837 and at one time was the county seat. Overall, the town appeared busy. I didn't notice any vacant buildings. Like most small towns I've seen, Sussex had a couple of bars, two restaurants that I noticed, a hardware store, and a clothing store. Red's Barber Shop had an old revolving striped pole out front.

As I continued through town, I entered a residential area of very nice, large, older homes. Just two blocks from the downtown the buildings of what must be Oglethorpe Christian College appeared. What a great setting, large oak trees and shaded walkways.

Finally, Oglethorpe Christian College.

Now to locate Draper Hall and Dr.Warren. The buildings here were very old. I would think most of them dated back to the turn of the century, some older yet. The larger, older buildings were red sandstone. Huge blocks. There was a nice campus square surrounded by four administration buildings or classroom buildings. The dormitories were located off the square. The enrollment here must be fairly small.

The sign on the corner of the square read:

Oglethorpe Christian College
Founded 1893
James T. Oglethorpe, Founder

Impressive.

I parked outside the administration building on the right of the square. The halls were a bit dark and echoed under foot. I tried to be quiet. A young coed manned the reception desk. Her name was Courtney. I asked her where I might find Draper Hall. Courtney pointed to a door at the end of the hall.

"Sir, if you go right out that door and across the lawn to the right, you'll see a sign for Ilfield Auditorium. Draper Hall is directly behind the auditorium. It's a small gray two-story building. Whose office are you looking for?"

I turned back to Courtney and answered, "Dr. Gabe Warren. He's expecting me."

"Your name, sir?"

"Oh, I'm sorry, Michael Carls from Moss University in Illinois."

"Mr. Carls, I'll call over to Dr. Warren's office and tell them to watch for you."

I just nodded and said, "Great."

It was only a two- or three-minute walk. The building, nestled off by itself away in the corner, just didn't seem to fit in with the rest of the campus.

As I approached the walkway leading to Draper Hall, I heard a friendly, "Hello, Mr. Carls."

The sight of a lanky young coed took me back with long, silky, black hair standing in the doorway. "Hi, you must be Samantha."

"Yes sir, Samantha Martinson, Dr. Warren's grad assistant. We spoke on the phone. How was your drive down?"

I reached out and shook her hand.

"The drive was fine, a bit longer than I thought, but just fine. Nice campus you have here."

Samantha smiled and said, "We like it. Kinda quaint. Come on in and I'll show you around."

Draper Hall was built in the mid 1950s. It resembled a typical sterile office building I'd seen before. The main floor was for classroom use. We walked to the end of the hall and down gray tiled stairs. Dr. Warren's office was off to the left. Nothing special. He had one computer, two desks, several old drab green file cabinets and a few chairs. A rather large avocado-colored refrigerator stood against one wall.

"Let me take your jacket," Samantha said, as she held out her hand. "You care for any coffee or a Coke?"

"No, no, I'm okay for now," I said, as I set my briefcase down next to my chair.

I watched Samantha as she walked to the coat rack. She reminded me of my niece Stephanie. She was tall, attractive, and very outgoing. *I think I'll like working with her,* I pondered.

As she turned, she must have caught me watching her.

"What? You're wondering why I like working in a place like this, digging into old dusty files and stuff? I think it's fun."

I laughed, "No, you're just not what I pictured as a grad assistant in history. You look like a fun-loving, free spirit, ready to tackle something far more exciting than lost Civil War soldiers."

"Well, Mr. Carls, maybe someday, but for now this is working out. By the way, I forgot to tell you that Gabe, I mean Dr. Warren, is in class for about another hour. Would you like a quick campus tour?"

We walked out of Draper Hall and into the square. Samantha pointed out the various buildings, their names, purposes, and a little history of each. She was well informed and had a great deal of energy in her voice. She said she came here to school instead of a larger state school because she simply loved the campus and its history.

Oglethorpe Christian College was originally the Old Soldiers Home. The oldest building, Farbeck Hall, was a hospital in 1855. After the Civil War, the state of Indiana bought the hospital and used it to house wounded veterans. In the years that followed, several more buildings were constructed to take care of old soldiers who had no families. The soldiers turned over their meager pension monies to the state in return for a place to call home. In 1893, the number of soldiers living in the home had dwindled to a point that the state could no longer afford to maintain the facility.

In that same year, a wealthy farm implement dealer and part-time minister bought the original four buildings from the state, established a Christian college, and named it after himself. That was, of course, James Oglethorpe. Samantha went on to say that over the years the school had been funded by various church denominations.

I gazed at the old buildings and marveled at the huge sycamore and oak trees that were in abundance. Samantha watched me taking in the entire campus splendor. "Pretty neat place, don't you think?" Samantha said with a feeling of satisfaction. Smiling, I nodded in agreement.

"This is quite a place, Samantha. No wonder you like it here," I said, as we turned the square. The air was starting to chill;

the temperature must have been around forty degrees. I could see dark clouds forming to the west. Could be snow moving in. Actually, it was nice for this time of year. Our February weather in northern Illinois was a good twenty degrees colder.

Samantha looked at her wristwatch and rather hurriedly said, "We better get back. Dr. Warren will be out of class in just a couple of minutes. He is very eager to meet you." With that said, we cut across the square and arrived at Draper Hall just as the bell ending classes rang. The students poured out of the classrooms and made their way out of the building.

From the bottom of the stairs, I could see a man about six feet tall standing just outside the office door. This had to be Gabe Warren. He was digging through his sport coat pockets trying to locate his keys. From behind me and in a clear voice, Samantha rang out, "I have my key, Dr. Warren."

Gabe Warren turned and looked over his glasses and caught me standing within five feet. "Well," he said, "you must be Mr. Carls. Come on in. I'm looking forward to working with you."

Samantha took her coat and mine and hung them on the coat rack. She turned and offered, "Anyone care for some coffee?" Before either of us could answer, Gabe suggested that we all go to the student center and have coffee or hot chocolate there. It was fine with me. Gabe picked up a file off his desk and then joined Samantha and me in bundling up and walking to the student center.

The center was located off the square and in the opposite direction from Draper Hall. The temperature was beginning to drop. We walked the nearly three hundred yards without saying very much. We were trying to stay warm. I noticed the wind from the west was gaining in intensity. Those dark clouds were really headed in our direction now. Sure looked like snow.

The student center was located on the ground floor of a women's dormitory. Inside, there were about fifty students in various stages, ranging from studying to sleeping. Most were just sitting having a beverage and talking to friends. From the looks I was getting as we entered, they knew I was a stranger on campus. To me, they appeared to be just like every other college student I've seen. The center itself was small, but comfortable; it fit into the campus aura.

After ordering our drinks at the counter, Gabe started the conversation by asking about my drive down. It was a natural icebreaker. I told him, as I had told Samantha earlier, that it took longer than I expected, but it went well. We found a round table in the corner.

Shortly after our drinks arrived, Gabe pulled out his file folder and opened it to the names of the twenty-three missing soldiers. "Let's start here," he said. Without taking a breath, he continued, "How would you like to divide up the list?" I was a little bewildered. I didn't think he wanted to jump into the project quite that fast.

I fumbled with my thoughts for a moment and then answered, "Dr. Warren, before we go any farther, why don't you let me explain what sources I have access to that may help us with the project?"

Focused in Samantha's direction, Dr. Warren said, "Fine, but please, call me Gabe, like everyone else around here does." Samantha shrugged her shoulders in reply. With the introductions out of the way, I continued to explain about the new computer access materials made available to us at Moss University.

I asked, "Gabe, have you read much about the ARPLANET system?"

Gabe's response was quick, "Of course I have. E-mail was invented in 1972! I understand that there has been some updating going on, but that material isn't available yet."

I went on to explain that the National Science Commission and the government, the military in particular, had combined resources and formed what is called telnet. This new system set standards and made it easier for nontechnical people to access libraries and other archival materials. We can now communicate through the network with other researchers and university colleagues around the world. We can share files and resources.

Gabe looked at me and summed up his thoughts in one word, "Wow!"

I continued by telling him about the development of the Wide Area Information Server (WAIS) site at Moss. WAIS had a full index of files in a database and allowed individual file searches by topic. Because of the vast amount of Civil War records in the National Archives, they became the guinea pig documents for the system. As I concluded, I said, "Believe it or not, the information we need, and that you could have used, is in those files. We have the files right in front of us!"

I had both Gabe and Samantha's undivided attention. They were awed. Samantha leaned toward Gabe and asked him, "Can we get that stuff here at Oglethorpe?"

Gabe just sat back and laughed, "Someday, Samantha, someday."

Gabe took a deep breath and said, "Okay, Mike, let's think about this. Where do you want to begin? You know this computer thing better than I do." I could see that Gabe was more interested now than ever before in pursuing the project. As I took a big sip of my hot chocolate, Samantha took a legal pad out of her bag. She reached over and picked up the paper from Gabe's file that had the names of the soldiers on it. She made two columns on the yellow sheet. At the top of one column, she wrote *Moss* and at the top of the second column she wrote *Oglethorpe*.

"Now," ordered Samantha, "how do you want to divide this list? I suggest we cut it right in half. Oglethorpe gets Ackley through Davidson, and Moss gets Franklin through Wollman. How does that sound?"

Gabe and I looked at each other and agreed with a simultaneous response, "Perfect!"

I briefly glanced around the room. The wall clock jarred my mind for a moment. "Excuse me," I said, "I have to check for someplace to stay tonight. I completely forgot."

"No problem, Mr. Carls," said Samantha; "there's a motel just outside of town on Route 129 South. It's called the Four Seasons Inn. Not much of an inn, but it should be okay. I'll get the phone number for you." Samantha went to the counter and asked the young lady working there for a phone book. Gabe and I continued to plan our research.

"Gabe, I'll check with my department head about setting up a satellite connection with your office. I also think I may be able to apply for a grant to pay Samantha to do most of the data collection. There are several different funding possibilities in the computer area. If we play this right, our project could be written off entirely by the National Science Commission."

Gabe was very amenable.

Samantha came back to the table and announced that a room was waiting for me at the Four Seasons Inn and that the room would be billed directly to Oglethorpe at a reduced rate. I thanked her as we gathered our coats and left the center to return to Gabe's office.

The walk back to Draper Hall seemed shorter than before. Returning always seemed shorter than going! The air was definitely colder. As we approached the walkway to Draper Hall, Gabe suggested we have lunch at Marilyn's Café at 1:30. I agreed, but I also wanted to get settled in my room and maybe freshen up before lunch. As I left Gabe and Samantha standing outside Draper Hall and headed for my car, I couldn't help but feel that I had somehow been sent here for a far more important mission than just finding out about Private Overland. Something felt very strange . . .

Samantha had been right in her assessment of Four Seasons Inn; it wasn't much of an inn. In its day it must have been a top-rated motel. That day was probably thirty years ago, however. The turquoise and white paint job was a real giveaway! The manager was an elderly man named Harry. As Harry led me to my room, he was pleased to inform me that the room was on the inside of the courtyard and poolside. I just smiled; I had no desire to swim in an outside pool in mid-February!

"Here we are, Mr. Carls, Room 105, poolside."

Harry handed me a single key on a plastic key chain.

"Thank you, Harry. I'm sure this will do just fine."

The room was dark with heavy vertical blinds. I opened the blinds to let in what light there was. The room was typical: a double bed with a dark blue comforter, night stands on either side of the bed, a small round table in the corner with one side chair. A long, double-drawer dresser was opposite the foot of the bed. A television sat on the dresser. A telephone was on the table. The bath was in the rear of the room.

I set my lone suitcase on the dresser next to the T.V. When I unzipped the suitcase, lying amongst my socks and underwear was a note from Marilyn.

I hope you find what you're looking for!

Love, Marilyn

I hope I do too, Marilyn!

The cold water felt refreshing on my face. I called Marilyn at work to let her know that I arrived okay and that I had met Dr. Warren. I could tell from her voice that she had worried about my drive. It had snowed all night in Illinois and several roads had been closed. I explained that there was no snow in Sussex and that only now snow clouds appeared on the horizon. The roads should be cleared by the time I drove home on Sunday.

Marilyn also said she had talked to Deanna and everything should be fine at the office and for me not to worry. Believe me, the office was the farthest thing from my mind right now.

I only had forty-five minutes until lunch at Marilyn's. I forgot to tell Marilyn about the café having her name. There will be plenty of time for that later.

As I sat on the edge of the bed, I picked up the remote for the T.V. There were only four channels, and two of those kept drifting in and out. I wasn't interested in a game show or the one soap opera. Channel 41, broadcasting out of Louisville, Kentucky, had a noon news show that was just about to end. The weather report was nearly over, but I caught enough to ascertain that southeastern Indiana was expecting 2-4 inches of snow by tomorrow morning. I hated driving in snow, especially on unfamiliar roads. I sat for about fifteen minutes and then decided I'd take my time heading back to town.

The drive back gave me another opportunity to see what Sussex had to offer. I had a little time to kill. There was a small industrial park just down the road and across from the motel. I noticed the sign at the entrance to the industrial sites listing all the tenants:

W. R. Whitney Press Barber Components
Fargo Ball Bearings Key-Line Plastics
Hasting Tool & Die Sabin Safety Hitches

Of those listed, it appeared to me that Whitney Press was the largest. This is quite an impressive industrial base for such a small town. I imagine most of the working 4,000 residents were employed here or at the college.

I parked across the street from Marilyn's. I was ten minutes early. I dropped two dimes in the parking meter in front of my car. A dime buys one hour's worth of parking in Sussex. Back home our meters start at twenty-five cents for thirty minutes. I really had stepped back in time!

The owner, Marilyn, greeted me at the door. The café seemed busy with a late lunch rush. I told her I was meeting some people and she immediately said, "Oh, you must be meeting Samantha Martinson and Dr. Warren. I reserved a table for you near the front window." She led me to a semicircular booth with deep cushions. As I slid into the booth, Marilyn asked if I wanted coffee.

"No, I'm coffeed out for the day, how about an ice tea?" As Marilyn left the booth, Samantha came in the door. She spotted me and came directly over.

"How is your room at Four Seasons?"

"It's fine. Cozy."

"Dr. Warren should be along in just a few minutes. He had to drop off some papers at administration."

"Tell me, Mr. Carls, why is this research so important to you?"

I waited to answer. Marilyn returned with my tea and asked Samantha if she wanted to order now or wait for Dr. Warren? Samantha ordered a soft drink.

I gave Samantha's inquiry another moment before responding. "Ya' know, Samantha, I started out doing this as a favor to a friend. He and I have been Civil War buffs for many years. It was Wes Wilson who brought me a copy of Gabe's article. However, I think this project may turn into something far more than finding Private Overland."

"Well," said Samantha, "I can tell you one thing for sure, Dr. Warren is really excited about whatever you have planned. He couldn't stop talking about the new computer connections you have and what that might mean in the future. He just went on and on. I think you made his day!"

No sooner had Samantha said that than Gabe Warren walked in.

"I see you had no problem finding our favorite place for lunch."

I scooted over and relied, "No problem at all; right in the heart of town."

Gabe put aside his menu and recommended any of the burger selections. He also suggested the house soups.

Marilyn started asking for our order even before she got to the table. "Hello, Doc, you want your usual Thursday special with a side of cole slaw? And what about you, Samantha?"

Gabe sat back and gave Marilyn a smile as he nodded in agreement. Samantha ordered a BLT and fries. I needed only to glean over the menu for a few seconds and decided on a Bleu Cheese burger, without onions.

"Doc, I'll bring you your coffee. You folks just settle back now. Food will be out in just a minute."

I took a deep breath as I looked at Gabe. "Back at the motel I was thinking just where this research might lead us. I have a lot of work on my desk from our teaching staff at Moss, but I can also apply for research time for special projects. I haven't done that in several years, but I see no reason why I can't now. If I can get a grant from the NSC, like I mentioned to you earlier, Gabe, we could do so much more. What do you say? Are you in with me?"

I could see that Gabe was in favor of the idea.

Samantha took a sip, swallowed, and said, "I plan on being here for a couple more years and I have no wedding plans for the next century, so why not?"

"Then good, that's what I'll do when I get back. It might take five or six months to get a reply from NSC. For now though, can I see some of your research, Gabe?"

Just as Gabe was about to answer, Marilyn came with our order; a good place to pause. After a much needed lunch, we headed back to the campus.

Back at Gabe's office, Samantha opened the top drawer of the old green file cabinet. The drawer was heavy with manila folders. There must have been a hundred or so. Samantha made four stacks of files on her desk. She knew these files inside and out and was the one who catalogued all the information for Gabe's doctoral research.

"Whatever you want to know, just ask. Everything here is hard copy!" Samantha was proud of her work.

"Aside from reading Gabe's dissertation, I'd like to know where you got this much information? Certainly not from the campus library."

"Of course not. Dr. Warren sent me to Indianapolis for two weeks to dig around in the state archives. Believe me, that was fun, but a lot of work. I came back with buckets of info. Those people have everything you can imagine—microfiche, newspapers, photos, diaries, pension records, discharges, whatever you need."

"Great, do you have any local historical societies or roundtable groups in the area? Sometimes they have personal records available that the state may not have."

"We tried to do some of that, but there was just too much. Do you think that maybe we missed some info on those soldiers?"

"It's possible that if we can track down these men one by one that we may be able to find them all. What about the county courthouse? Did you get much from them?"

"Some, but not much. It seems that most of the 14th Indiana came from surrounding counties or over the border from Kentucky. You know Kentucky was a neutral state, right?

Well, if a man wanted to enlist, he had to go somewhere else. We think that several of the men in the 14th did just that."

"I see no other way of going about this. Our search is going to have to be broad. What do you think, Gabe?"

"I agree," Gabe said with a sigh. "I know I have time for this, but do you?"

I let Gabe's comment sink in. I knew it could be extensive, but I also knew that this was something I really wanted to do. Wes would be elated just to find out about Private Overland. Now it seemed there was so much more to do!

"Gabe, I'll apply for the project time and grant. My assistant's name is Deanna Hovland. Samantha, you're going to get to know her real well. You two should work well together. Now, Samantha, why don't you show me the first files you have there?"

As Gabe sat at his desk preparing for tomorrow's classes, Samantha and I reorganized the files into workable tasks. The first pile dealt with the history of the 14th Indiana volunteer Infantry. Next were fifteen files containing information on the members of the regiment. I thought that there had to be more data. Samantha reminded me that Gabe only used this information to compile the magazine article. He didn't need very detailed material. His dissertation concerned pensions for Indiana Veterans. I understood the difference right away. I thought that it would be best to take these first fifteen files and break them down by name and to identify where each man had come from.

Where did he live? Where did he enlist? What was his pre-enlistment occupation? Was he married? There where so many questions. Our job now was to find an equal number of answers! I joked that we should go down to the local hardware store and buy some shovels—we were going to be doing a lot of digging.

The afternoon hours melted away. It was 5 o'clock before I knew it. Samantha and I had purged several dozen files. Quite frankly, I had seen enough for one day. Everything was beginning to look alike.

I noticed Gabe was looking fairly beat. "Gabe," I said, "let's call it a day and have some dinner. Sound good?" Gabe put down his plan book and sighed in agreement.

"I think I'm too tired for dinner tonight. Why don't you and Samantha have dinner on me? Samantha knows my favorite place near Mount Sterling. It's only a twelve- or -thirteen mile drive, just down the road. Great steaks! You two have a good time. Samantha will have plenty of questions I'm sure; she always does."

Gabe packed his briefcase with papers to grade at home. Samantha proceeded to arrange the files on her desk in neat stacks according to their subject matter. I could see her housekeeping was very well organized. No wonder Gabe kept her here.

On the way out of the building, Samantha offered to drive to dinner. She asked, "Do you need to stop by the Four Seasons before we head out of town; it's on the way?"

I thought for just a second and said, "Not really."

"Okay then, my car is right around the side of the auditorium. A yellow Beetle."

I've heard it said that a person's car is a reflection of the owner's personality. That is certainly a correct statement in Samantha's case. A yellow Volkswagen Beetle was just perfect for her.

"I haven't been in a Beetle in twenty years," I said as I forced my forty-eight-year-old body into the passenger seat.

We followed Route 129 out of town and into the open country. It was already dark. The clouds that threatened snow earlier must have blown over. The stars were bright on what had become a full moon night. The landscape was peaceful.

Our dinner at Fuller's was very good, just as Gabe had said it would be. I particularly enjoyed the atmosphere—quiet, rustic, and nicely decorated in a country motif. Pleasant.

Samantha was a most gracious hostess. Our conversation was not only about research and history, but about family as well. I told her how Marilyn had encouraged me to do this alone and enjoy myself. We also discussed my friend Wes and his interest in the Civil War.

Samantha had come from a family of teachers. Her father was an English teacher in Columbus, Ohio. Her mother had taught for seventeen years before she passed away in 1982. Her brother teaches architecture in Japan.

I told Samantha that tomorrow I wanted to drive into Vevay, the county seat, to check their records. She suggested that since we were so close that we drive by the courthouse tonight so that I would know exactly where to go tomorrow. It was only a ten-minute drive from Fuller's.

Vevay is an old river town with large houses and huge yards. These mansions were probably built by merchants who owned barges on the Ohio River. The hilly terrain here was very different from Sussex.

The county courthouse was an old redbrick three-story structure located in the center of the town square. It was apparent that in recent years the county needed to expand its facilities. Three modern stone buildings housing the correctional center, the county records center, and the county legislative center, were located across the square within walking distance. We parked the car in front of the records center and I walked up to the front door to see what hours the building was open. I was in luck. The sign read, Monday thru Friday, 8:30 to 4:30. I knew where I'd be spending my Friday!

Samantha dropped me off at the Four Seasons Inn about 9:00. It had been and enjoyable evening. I told her I would stop by the office when I returned from Vevay. I called Marilyn and told her what a busy day I had had. She went on about the snow in Illinois and about digging out the driveway by herself. I told her that if I didn't find much in Vevay that I might leave for home on Saturday instead of Sunday. I would see how things went tomorrow. We said good night.

I pulled into the same parking spot Samantha and I had used the night before. I was early. I had fifteen minutes to find a cup of coffee. Across the street was the Courthouse Café. It was quite ironic. I merely mentioned that I was waiting for the records center to open and the man sitting next to me at the counter replied that he was the records room manager. His name was Gene Fife. We talked briefly about what records I was interested in. Gene said he knew of some material that may be of interest. He also remembered Samantha doing research for Dr. Warren's article. He seemed to think that there was more information than Samantha had wanted. I was eager to see what Gene could find for me. It sounded like a positive start.

The records room was similar to other such rooms I had seen. It was organized, yet cluttered and very historical. Gene, like most archivists, knew exactly where to retrieve old papers, files, and manuscripts. He reached over the top of a large storage cabinet and handed me an enormous brown box. It was a waxed box, old and dusty. On the top of the box was penciled:

Civil War 1861-65
Soldiers, Discharges, Diaries

My eyes jumped out of my head. It couldn't be this easy!

"Gene," I said as if in shock, "did Samantha Martinson see this box?"

"Yes, of course she did."

34

"Did she find what she was looking for?"

"I think so. She didn't say she didn't."

I remember thinking to myself, *what else could be in the box that a researcher like Samantha might have missed?* There was only one way to find out—open it up and have a look.

I had my list of missing soldiers. Gene pointed to a large table off to one corner. "You can camp out here till 4:30 if you want. If you need something else, just ask. I'm sure I can find it if we have it."

I thanked Gene as I opened the dusty, frail box. The smell of musk filled the air. Samantha must not have had this box open very long. The papers on top were in order by date and by name. I figured that was Samantha's doing. Very organized! I removed everything from the box. Some of the papers nearly crumbled in my hand. *Careful, Mike.*

I made three distinct piles on the table. Material related to soldiers' names, diaries, and discharges were of primary concern. They were right in front of me. Newspaper articles were by themselves to the right. Miscellaneous papers and such were on my left. There wasn't much room left for me to work at the table. I put the newspapers back in the box for now. I set my list of soldiers from the 14th Indiana on the table and tried to memorize their names in alphabetical order.

The first name on my list was Private Edgar Franklin, Company E. The only mention of Franklin was on the roster for the company and that he had been mustered in on May 12, 1861, in Terre Haute. Franklin was born in Switzerland County in 1838, but no specific day was given. Upon entering the service, Franklin listed his occupation as a farmer. I thought I was on to something right away. However, the only other information on Private Franklin was that he had fought at Cold Harbor in June of 1864. Nothing was mentioned after that date. No wonder Samantha listed him as one of the missing. I started to think maybe there could be another angle to Franklin; he couldn't have just disappeared.

Rather than dig into too much at one time, I thought it best to concentrate on one or two veterans for now. Another trip to Sussex and Vevay was always possible. Franklin would be a good start.

The next name on my list was Frederick Gale, Private, Company K. I must have been lucky with my first try; not so with Frederick Gale. I assumed that meant he was from another county, not Switzerland. I suppose the next step in finding anything regarding Private Gale would either be on my computer back at Moss or a stop at the state archives in Indianapolis. I tried to match up several more names with those listed in the records for Switzerland County. I found two, David Hayes and Hiram Oats. Both were born in 1840 and were from Moorefield, Indiana, about five miles north of Vevay on Route 129. If nothing else, I could stop there on my way back to Sussex. Who knows, there may be some family still in the area. There may be some church records available as well.

As I laid the papers for Hayes and Oats aside, I picked up a rather unusual looking folded document. I hadn't seen anything like this in a long time. The document was about two inches wide and only four or so inches in height. The material felt like leather, but it wasn't leather. It was called buff paper. This kind of paper product was used for only the most important documents, most notably birth or death certificates. I unfolded the pages carefully. The writing was done in ink and it was nearly invisible from age. It read:

Conscripts and Transfers

Bendalone, J	14th inf	70th inf	July 19,64
Tidall, H	14th inf	43rd inf	July 19,64
Wollman, W	14th inf	27th inf	July 19,64
Watson, L	33rd inf	27th inf	July 20,64
Meadows, B	19th inf	23rd artl	Aug 11,64
Mason, H	9th cav	15th cav	Nov 12,65
Oats, H	14th inf	27th inf	July 19,64

| Dix, C | 14th inf | 70th inf | July 19,64 |
| Alt, B | 14th inf | 70th inf | July 22,64 |

Entered: James K. Rhodes, Adj. Gen. State of Indiana

This was incredible! How could Samantha have failed to notice this? Right in front of her were the names of at least six of the soldiers listed as missing in Gabe's article. They weren't missing; they either transferred to another unit or they got paid by someone to fight in that person's name under a conscript. Samantha either had no idea what a conscript was or perhaps she never opened the document. I was having a ball. It felt terrific to find this kind of information. I was sure the rest of the search wouldn't be this easy. I was right!

In order to find out what happened to the soldiers that transferred to other units, it would be necessary to research the histories of those particular units individually. It would take time, but it certainly could be done. I looked forward to the challenge. This was getting very exciting. To a researcher like me, this was like opening King Tut's tomb!

I asked Gene if I could make copies of the items from the box. He had no objections. I carefully put the small tri-fold under the top of the copier. I pressed down lightly. The greenish copy beam flashed under the document. The printed form was nearly black. Reading it was impossible. I managed to copy eighteen other pages of information from this one source. Outstanding.

Gene had been busy gathering other materials for me while I was reading and copying from the waxed box. He had several original diaries and family histories that had been donated to the records collection over the years. I knew I wouldn't have time to go through all that Gene had. I asked if it would be possible to set these items aside until I could come back and review them.

"Of course I can set them aside; no one ever asks for this stuff anymore. I'll create a space for you on a shelf over here." With that, Gene opened a steel gray cabinet and placed an armful of papers on the second shelf. "Here, this is your shelf now. I'll label it with your name. If you come back and I'm not here, they'll know this is here for you, sound okay?" I thanked Gene. What a nice gesture. I knew that this would save me a lot of time looking for records when I do come back. I couldn't thank Gene enough.

How the time flies. I glanced at my watch, 2:45. I hadn't stopped since Gene unlocked the door at 8:30. I felt horrible keeping Gene from lunch. I hurriedly suggested that I treat him to lunch at the Courthouse Café. Gene looked surprised. "Nonsense, let's go to my house. Dorothy can whip up something for us. She enjoys the company, and besides, we can talk some more about this research of yours." How could I say no?

Gene's house was a modest brick bungalow. "Welcome to the ole homestead," Gene said rather proudly. "Raised three boys here; bought the place in 1964. It was a tight fit with the boys here, but now that they're grown and on their own, it's just the right size for Dot and me."

Dorothy Fife was a pleasant and gracious lady. She was very quiet, matronly, and content with her place life. She took a great deal of pride in her home. The lunch she prepared so unexpectedly was fabulous. I guess eating all your meals out makes one appreciate a good home-cooked meal. Our conversation was centered on my research and the usual small talk. Dorothy had grown up in the area. Gene was originally from Cincinnati. They had met in the fifties. Dorothy had moved to Cincinnati with a girlfriend and had worked for a shirt manufacturer. Gene was a shift supervisor at the same company. As Gene would say, "One thing led to another, which led to three sons."

I could see that they enjoyed having guests in their home. I was just about to comment that I had to be leaving, when Dorothy offered their house for my stay when I come back to Vevay. Again, how could I say no, especially to Dorothy? She reminded me so much of my own mother.

It was 4 o'clock when I said my good-byes and promised to keep in touch with Gene and Dorothy. It was real fate that brought Gene and me together. I could foresee us spending many hours together in the future, researching and enjoying Dot's cooking.

The late Friday afternoon rush hour on Route 129 in southeastern Indiana was quite different than what I was used to back home. I think there were three other cars on the road all the way back to Sussex. I drove through the small cluster of homes that made up Moorefield. There was no business district; mainly a farming community. The only church in town, Southern Methodist, was locked up tight. Office hours ended at 3:00 on Fridays. I would have to make it a point to stop by again on my next trip.

The heat in my room at the Four Seasons was overwhelming. Harry must have been in doing the housekeeping and turned it up. Granted, it was forty degrees outside, but eighty degrees inside was a bit much. I called Gabe's office. Samantha answered and said Gabe had left for the day. "So Mr. Carls, how was your day in Vevay?"

I began to tell Samantha what I had found when she interrupted me and suggested that we meet at Marilyn's Café in an hour. I agreed. That would give me time to shower and relax a few minutes. I called Marilyn in Sycamore. She was about to head home. I told her I would spend the night in Sussex and probably head home by late morning. She said the snow shouldn't be a problem; the streets were clear and it hadn't snowed since Thursday. I told her briefly about my day and said I'd call her later before bedtime.

Samantha was studying the menu when I arrived at Marilyn's. I told her about Gene and that I had just eaten lunch at 3:00. Food was not something I needed right now, but coffee was in order. Samantha ordered a country-fried steak dinner. I thought I'd talk while she ate! That's how it went for the next forty-five minutes.

I asked her about the waxed box at the records center. She didn't remember seeing the tri-fold document as I described it. Strange. Something like that is hard to forget. Could it be that it wasn't in the box six months ago when Samantha did her research? Although it didn't seem likely, I would have to discuss that with Gene the next time we talked.

I asked Samantha if she had studied anything about the use of a "conscripted" soldier. She said that she honestly couldn't remember. It was obvious she hadn't studied about them or that she had forgotten. I explained that during the Civil War a gentleman could pay someone else, usually a veteran, to fight in his place for a $300 fee. The buyer then had his name removed from the draft rolls. That was a great deal of money at that time. It has been estimated that nearly fifty thousand northern men opted for conscription service. It was all completely legal. In several cases, the veteran soldiers took the money and fled to the neighboring county and conscripted under a different name, collecting several "fees" at the same time. Civil War records can be faulty with names of soldiers who actually never fought at all. When these guys were caught, they were likely to be sent directly to the front lines of battle, sometimes even without a gun.

I noticed the gold bracelet dangling from Samantha's left wrist. Either I hadn't seen it before, or I just didn't notice it. I was instantly reminded of the gold watch Wes had sent along with me. How dumb of me to forget about it. I asked if she minded finishing dinner while I ran back to the motel to get something to show her. Of course it was okay; however, her curiosity was really aroused!

It only took me fifteen minutes or so to make the round trip from Marilyn's. I placed the watch in Samantha's hand. She looked at it with awe, saying very slowly, "Wow, where did you get this?"

I explained that Wes had given it to me to show Gabe. I asked her if the date meant anything to her based on her research of the 14th Indiana Regiment. Samantha continued to toy with the watch, but said nothing as she pondered the inscription. Then, as if a light popped on in her head, she said, "Yes, 1871, I do have something on that. It's in the office. Let's run by there after I finish eating.

Draper Hall was a dark and eerie place after hours. Samantha pulled her office keys from her coat pocket, dropping one leather glove in the process. I retrieved the glove. Samantha hastily tossed her coat on Gabe's chair as we entered the office and started ruffling through stacks of green file folders on her desktop. It didn't take her long to find what she was looking for.

Samantha unfolded an old newspaper and said with great satisfaction in her voice, "Here it is, December 17, 1871, tenth anniversary of the forming of the 14th Indiana. The reunion was held in Indianapolis. I knew I had seen that date somewhere." I was pleased and surprised at the same time. Great. At least now we know what that was all about.

But what happened to Private Overland after the reunion? What other information did Samantha have in her file that was not included in Gabe's article? I could see newspaper clippings and an array of notes in that file alone.

I reached over and grabbed a handful of files, perhaps eight or ten. I asked Samantha if I could take them back to the motel and sort through them. Then I could relax in the quiet of my room. That's how I work.

I told Samantha that I wanted to be leaving for Illinois before noon the next day. I would drop the files off to her either here at the office, or someplace else, like Marilyn's, on my way out of town. We agreed to meet at Marilyn's around 9:00 for a late breakfast.

The parking space I had been using at the Four Seasons was occupied by a moving van. I drove around the side of the building and found the last remaining spot. The motel was full. What could be going on in Sussex on a Friday night?

After getting ready for bed, I spread the files out on the bed and I turned on the television, mainly out of habit. I didn't care what was on. The volume was off. There were at least a dozen magazine and newspaper clippings in the first three files I opened. Nothing out of the ordinary, articles about battles in which the regiment had fought, biographies, and obituaries. No mention of any of the soldiers on Gabe's list.

As I was about to close the file for the night, I noticed an advertisement in the lower left-hand corner of one of the newspaper pages. The ad was for horse rosettes and bridle supplies at Bean's Hardware Store in Aberdeen. Aberdeen was a small town directly east of Sussex, about seven or eight miles. Could this Bean be Thomas Bean from Company A?

The date on top of the page was November 14, 1873. I opened my Official Indiana Road Map and looked for Aberdeen. Sure enough, there it was, east of Sussex, but in Ohio County. If Gabe wanted additional information on Private Bean, he would have to check in Ohio County records, assuming this was our Mr. Bean. I marked the ad and scribbled some notes for Samantha to follow up on. This would be a good starting point for her in our search.

I went through the remaining files, but found nothing. It was a freak accident that I had seen Bean's ad. Overlooking something like that can happen to even the best of researchers. I called Marilyn at 9:00. She was just about to give up on me calling and go to bed. She'd had a rough week at work. I told her I would be leaving Sussex before noon and to expect me home by this time tomorrow night. It had been a long day for me as well.

I gave Samantha the files at breakfast. She was eager to get started on her and Gabe's list. She said she would try to make arrangements to go to Ohio County and look up Mr. Bean. I had said my good-byes and was on my way home. The drive towards Indianapolis went well. I would stop at the state archives on another trip. My destination now was home and my own bed.

Near Champaign, Illinois, I couldn't help but notice the frost clinging to the trees. It was beautiful—White snow, blue skies, white trees, peaceful harmony. I always enjoyed driving alone; it gave me time to think. I had learned a great deal over the past two days. I couldn't imagine what mysteries we might unlock in the future.

♣ ♣

Chapter 3

"Do not protect yourself by a fence, but rather by your friends."

Czech Proverb

Saturday night at home in Sycamore usually meant relaxing and watching television. Marilyn cuddled up on one sofa while I did the same on the other. We both liked to cap off winter nights with a hot chocolate. It was home and I had missed it. Marilyn and I rarely spent time apart.

Monday morning found me at work and back to reality. Deanna had finished things up for me last week, but a new list of projects beckoned my attention. Joanne Darling wasn't going to let me off the hook much longer. I had a note from Deanna saying that Dr. Darling had a new graduate assistant. His name was David Hinman and he had previously worked in the natural history field. Although I hadn't met him, my first thought was that he could pick up some of the work Dr. Darling was requesting. I may have the opportunity for a bit of free time to do some of my own research!

By the end of the week I made plans to investigate the grant-writing process for the National Science Commission. Applying for research time from the department would be no problem, as long as I documented the need and had my project fully organized. I started getting all my ducks in a row.

Work was going well. I hadn't heard from my colleagues at Oglethorpe in nearly two months. I wondered how they were doing and I decided to call. I had done what I could on my end for now. The grant request had been submitted and my project plan was waiting on my desk.

Samantha answered the phone. I could tell she was short of breath. She had just left the office and was halfway up the stairs when she heard the phone ringing. She had rushed back downstairs.

"Hi, Samantha, this is Mike Carls. How are things down there? I haven't heard a squeak from you guys. Is everything alright?"

"Yes, yes, Mr. Carls, everything's just fine. You know, busy and such. I did manage to get over to Ohio County."

"Fine. How is Dr. Warren doing?"

Samantha seemed to pause for a second. Then, in a much more serious tone she added, "He's been very sick, pneumonia. I've been holding down the fort here and teaching all his classes for almost three weeks now. I've tried to do some work on Private Bean, but I don't really have the time."

I took in all that Samantha had said. It was obvious that she thought she had to please me. Before she could say another word, I cut her off. "Whoa, Samantha, there is no rush on any of this. You just do what you have to do for now. The research can wait. Can I help you in any way? You sound like you have a full plate. Are you getting any help from other faculty?"

Samantha took a deep breath. She was under a great deal of stress. I knew this young lady had a lot of self-confidence and suggested she step back, take a look at the big picture and then break her tasks down into smaller pieces. She immediately understood.

"Thank you, Mr. Carls. I wish you were here to help. I guess I'm trying to do it all. Dr. Warren will be fine in a week or so. I never realized how much he really does here. I should have known. How are you doing?"

I told her about the grant application for the project and about my proposal. Other than that, things were as usual, busy on my end too. I asked Samantha to call when she could and we would talk more about the project.

I called Samantha a couple of weeks later and found her in much better spirits. Gabe was back on his feet and normalcy had returned to Oglethorpe. I was much relieved for Samantha. She was quite trooper and Gabe was lucky to have her there.

The National Science Commission had certainly taken their time considering my grant proposal. It had been four months since I submitted the forms. Finally, a response. I held the envelope for a couple of minutes before I could bolster the courage to open it. It was one of those moments in your life that meant everything. I would have to compare it to saying "I do" or getting a letter from the I.R.S.

Slowly, I tore the side of the envelope open. Yes! Our project was approved. I read on. I had requested $5,000. The joy I felt was overwhelming! Not only was the project approved, but also a master grant of $35,000 had been provided for computer hook-ups and site development. Samantha and Gabe had to hear the news. I called Marilyn at work. I was somewhat surprised at her jubilant response. Marilyn knew how much this meant to me. We were going to celebrate in style. No home cooking tonight! Next I had to call Samantha and Gabe.

Samantha's scream nearly blew out my eardrum. Gabe reacted likewise. They were ecstatic! Oglethorpe Christian College had never been involved in anything remotely resembling what we were about to do. We all felt very, very good.

We also realized that now the work would begin. We needed to have a meeting with all the parties involved and formulate a timetable and a plan of action. The excitement was building.

I invited Gabe and Samantha to come to Sycamore and Moss University. They would stay at our home. Marilyn insisted. I would coordinate everything on my end. I thought that Deanna and Samantha would need some time together. They would be working very closely over the next couple of years. I would also have to clear things with Dr. Darling for the use of David Hinman. She kept him fairly busy. David was a sharp young man. He was a bit geeky in a good way, but he knew his stuff. He could do the work; it was coming into our slow season in the research department anyway.

Our first planning meeting got underway in July of 1987. It was an exceptionally hot July. Gabe and Samantha drove up in her Volkswagen. Marilyn and I waited patiently for their arrival. Marilyn had made a small feast of favors and snacks for the perfect afternoon welcome. She had something very special planned for dinner. The two spare bedrooms were awaiting their guests. Everything was right. Marilyn had overseen things to the final detail. She loved to entertain and it showed.

As if on cue, Samantha pulled into our driveway at exactly 2 o'clock. Gabe stepped out of the car and stretched his cramped body. It had been a long drive. Marilyn and I gathered up the five pieces of luggage, which seemed like a lot for a five-day stay. No matter, they were in Sycamore and we were all excited about the work ahead. Marilyn and Samantha had already taken to each other. They immediately talked up a storm that continued for the entire stay, almost like a mother-daughter reunion. It was if they had known each other all their lives.

Gabe and I chatted about the project as we enjoyed Marilyn's relishes and dips. No need for an icebreaker here; good food does it every time. Samantha was on a house tour with Marilyn. We had remodeled our old house and Marilyn enjoyed showing it off. The house was built in the late nineteen hundreds. It had taken us twenty-five years to finish the updating, but it was finally done.

At the end of their tour, the ladies joined us on the back deck. Samantha eagerly sampled Marilyn's relish tray. The pool sparkled under the July sun. Samantha looked forward to a relaxing, late-night swim. Finally, we all gathered around the glass-topped patio table with our plates of refreshments. I had great news to share with our guests.

Marilyn joined in our conversation about the project and the grant money. She wanted to be part of the adventure and I welcomed her interest and enthusiasm. None of us realized what a wonderful, fulfilling journey this would become. For now, we were enjoying the moment and sharing a beautiful summer afternoon.

I let Gabe and Samantha settle in. I asked them if they had had any luck finding anyone on their list. Samantha had followed her lead on Private Bean, but it led her to a dead end. Gabe said he contacted a researcher in Daviess County Indiana about Private James Blocker. He gathered what might turn out to be conclusive evidence that Blocker had died in a private hospital in 1893. Gabe had gone beyond his original research. He had requested county death records from six counties surrounding Terre Haute. On one of those lists was James Blocker, Union veteran and hardware merchant. His death certificate mentions his widow, Sarah, and three sons, all of Washington, Indiana. Things were progressing faster than any of us had imagined.

I looked at Gabe with great satisfaction. He caught my look and asked me, "What's that look for?" I couldn't hold back any longer. Marilyn knew what I was going to say. Marilyn smiled and reached for Samantha's hand. Samantha glanced at me with a puzzled look. I told them both that about a month earlier I had located two of the soldiers on my list.

Both Gabe and Samantha burst into laughter. "Great," said Gabe, "how did you do that so fast? Where on earth did you get your information?" It was rewarding to see them so happy.

I went on to explain that the ARPLANET system at Moss could do wonders. I searched pension records, discharge records, and several regimental histories. One of the soldiers, Hiram Oats, had transferred to the 27th Indiana Infantry Regiment and had participated in the occupation of Atlanta with the 20th Corps under General Sherman. Oats was accidentally killed in the demolition of railroad cars three weeks after his transfer. His service records indicated his rank as Private and his "transfer" date as July 19, 1864. There was no mention of his enlistment in the 14th Indiana. I have to assume that this Hiram Oats was the same man. The transfer date was the key. Only the enlisting officer of the 27th Indiana could only answer why his previous service in the 14th was not mentioned. He either forgot to do so, or perhaps he thought it didn't matter at such a late date in the war.

Gabe was spellbound. "You found all that on a file in the computer?"

"Yes, Gabe, and there's more. I also located the family of Horace Tidall. It's a rare name in the United States. I ran the name though a census screen of all white pages listed on the computer and it located nine Tidall households in the country. Believe it or not, three of them still live in Indiana. Marshall Tidall is the great-grandson of Horace. He lives in South Bend. He even sent me a picture of Horace's grave in Mt. Carmel Cemetery. Horace was lost in the records because he conscripted under a different name when he reenlisted in the 43rd Indiana Infantry. He survived the war and died at the age of eighty-seven in 1928."

I had told them I had some great connections here at Moss! Now Gabe realized just what I meant. This was going to be a most rewarding adventure. Samantha was overjoyed and gave Marilyn a huge hug. It was a tremendous way to start our five days together. Our spirits were high and our camaraderie was firm. We had the drive and the means to accomplish our goal. It was midsummer and the sun was high.

Our guests went to their rooms to unpack as I helped Marilyn clean up the deck and put the leftovers in the fridge. I could see she was having a good time. As I wiped the dishes, I asked her how she liked my Indiana friends. She always thought researchers were eggheads and geeks.

She just smiled and said, "They're great; really nice people. Gabe and Samantha should think about getting together. They make a cute couple." *Oh no,* I thought, *she isn't going to play matchmaker!*

Gabe came downstairs and sat in the living room. I told him to prop up his feet and relax. He looked comfortable. Without saying a word, I tossed him the remote for the T.V. We men understood certain things without wasting words.

Samantha came into the kitchen and asked Marilyn if she could shower and lie down for a while before dinner. Marilyn was the perfect hostess as she showed her where the extra towels were and assured her that we wouldn't eat without her. The house was quiet.

Marilyn had planned a neighborhood cookout for the evening meal, a potluck dinner. She thought it would be an excellent way for Gabe and Samantha to meet my colleagues from the university. She was right, of course. Better to meet here than in a stuffy office. As they say, behind every good man there's a great woman. I wonder what my mother-in-law would say about that?

Samantha wore a beautiful summer dress with a large green flower print. It was an ideal choice with her long black hair. Her sandals and small white pearl necklace completed the perfect picture. Gabe, like me, wore a polo style shirt and khaki shorts. We were dressed for the weather. Marilyn looked lovely, as always, in white Bermuda shorts, a red sleeveless top and white sandals. Her light brown hair was cut three inches off the shoulder and turned in. I was very proud of her. At age forty-five she was still a very attractive woman and she looked far younger than her years.

As each guest and neighbor arrived, I introduced Gabe and Samantha. Marilyn had briefed everyone about our project and about Gabe and Samantha's role. Dr. Darling, her husband, Douglas, and David Hinman came as surprise guests. I had only met Douglas Darling once before, and that was at a formal university function. He was an electrician by trade. Douglas didn't say much, but I doubt if he could anyway with a wife like Joanne. She dominated the house, at least from what I could tell. It only seemed proper that if I was going to be handing over much of the research duties to David, that Joanne Darling should see the reason why. She was taking this whole affair very well. The university had granted me a one-year leave for this research.

Both the evening and the food were wonderful. Gabe, Samantha, and I were congratulated over and over by my friends and neighbors. Gabe and Samantha felt right at home.

After an early breakfast of Marilyn's fine cooking, it was time to show off our computer mainframe at Moss. Gabe and Samantha were equally excited. Marilyn had to be at work at 9:00 but would join us for lunch.

Gabe grabbed his briefcase as we left the house. Samantha marveled at the size of the campus and the number of buildings. I told her our enrollment was just under twenty-seven thousand undergraduates. She sat in awe. Gabe seemed to take it all in. He had completed his undergraduate degree at Indiana State and had experienced a big school before. If he was impressed, he didn't show it.

I parked the car in front of my building Jeffrey Hall, named for Charles Jeffrey, an early founder of Sycamore and financier of the university. I thought it a typical old university building. It had been built in 1921. My office was on the second floor. There were four cubicles in our research department.

Deanna Hovland was waiting for us as we walked in. "Welcome to research heaven. I'm Deanna. You must be Samantha and you Dr. Warren. I've heard all about you two from Dr. Carls. Everything! He has been waiting for this day since he first read your article. Isn't it amazing how all this has unfolded?" Deanna was so full of energy. "I can't wait to show you around. The new Internet system is really great."

Samantha stared at Gabe and then turned to Deanna, "You said *Dr.* Carls. He's a doctor?"

Deanna just squinted back at her with, "Sure. He has been for twenty years. He doesn't go by doctor; he just prefers Mr. Carls."

It was cool as Deanna led our guests into the glass-enclosed, temperature-controlled computer room. The nine large blue IBM mainframes lined the outer wall. They hummed in a gentle moan, their tape reels clicking in harmony.

The latest updates had been made so the research and file sharing capabilities were far more expanded from just a couple of months ago. The whole computer generation was in constant change. These were exciting times.

Deanna explained that there were fewer than fifty sites like ours in the entire country. The National Science Commission had funded the development of NSCNet in 1986 and we had that system here at Moss. The computer commands were now standardized and we could communicate via the Internet with colleagues in various departments like engineering and physics, as well as libraries and other outside resources. With the grant from the National Science Commission, we should be able to set up a smaller, but similar system at Oglethorpe. It would allow us to communicate daily as we go.

Deanna and I spent the entire morning introducing Gabe and Samantha to the computer system. Hands-on is the only way to learn this technology. Samantha really got into it and was having a ball. Gabe took his turn at the computer as well. I think he realized that Samantha would be the one entering most of the data and searching files. He was satisfied to sit back and let her learn it all. Deanna was enjoying the opportunity to show off the system and her expertise. It was good for her.

Deanna and Samantha were a good match. I could tell that the four of us would work well together. We were of one mind with a common goal, to use the latest technology to locate and bring closure to the hunt for the last twenty lost Indiana Civil War soldiers.

The week seemed to be flying by. All of us had explored new frontiers. Marilyn had made some fantastic meals. She was a wonderful hostess. We shared some good times. Our house hasn't felt such joy in a long time. We had to have a send-off party of some kind. Marilyn would take care of that.

Marilyn made reservations at Billington's Inn for dinner on Gabe and Samantha's final night in Sycamore. Deanna would be joining us for the evening. The short drive to Billington's was made especially memorable because of the bright, summer sky that evening. Red and green streaks of light filled the sky. It was quite a show. Perhaps it was a sign!

It was decided, for now, to keep the list of soldiers we each had. Each team, Samantha and Gabe, and Deanna and I, would work independently of each other but stay in touch and share information as it became available. Gabe still had classes to teach and Samantha had her job to assist him with her normal schedule of duties. I had a year of time to dedicate to the project, plus Deanna's assistance.

At dinner we discussed the fact that pension files and discharge records were becoming more and more accessible to the public. There had always been an interest in these documents. The surge of people doing personal genealogies was at an all-time high. Gabe and Samantha had a basic understanding of our system and its seemingly unlimited capabilities. What we could find with this new technology remained to be seen. We had exchanged e-mail addresses and established a checklist to assist in a coordinated effort. We were on the same track.

The night passed quickly. Saying good-bye to good friends is always hard to do. Marilyn had such a wonderful time with Samantha. The two of them had shopped and talked feverishly all week. They had become very close. It was good for both of them. We planned on getting together again in the late fall, before Thanksgiving if possible. Gabe would pick the place to meet; a halfway point would be ideal. A final toast to the project ended the evening. Our guests had a long drive ahead of them in the morning.

Gabe and Samantha woke early and had a breakfast of ham, sausage, hash browns, and scrambled eggs. Marilyn wouldn't let anyone leave the house hungry. I helped Gabe pack the VW. With the purchases made by Samantha and Marilyn, it was a tight fit. Once they were on their way at 8:30, Marilyn and I retired to the house. Rest. It's always nice to have company, but it is exhausting. Marilyn left me on the patio with my coffee while she went about stripping the beds and doing other laundry. It was back to normal at the Carls' house.

When I entered the office Monday morning I saw that I had an e-mail waiting for me. I figured it was from Gabe saying they had gotten to Sussex okay. They hadn't phoned Saturday night or all day Sunday. I was quite surprised to read a message from a Krista Butler. Somehow she had heard about our project and was inquiring about it. I also made note of the suffix on her address, *.gov.* Program identity designations had been established since 1979. Our identity suffix was *.edu.* The general public and companies used *.com* or *.org.* I hadn't seen a *.gov* inquiry before. Who was this Krista Butler, and what interest could she have in our research?

I replied to Miss Butler's e-mail, asking how she had heard of the project and if she was equally interested in Civil War research. The response I received was somewhat alarming and I became suspicious of her intentions. Her reply to me was crisp and to the point.

> To: MCarlsRES@Ilnet.edu
> From: KBUTLER@FstNET.gov
> Subject: Civil War soldiers
>
> Mr. Carls,
>
> I am not particularly interested in Civil War research, just in who is doing research on Civil War soldiers. I was made aware of your research by a mutual grant writing organization. It all involves a project that I am sure we will discuss as time goes on.
>
> Krista Butler

I was completely baffled. Who could the *mutual* organization be? The people of the National Science Commission were the only ones who knew of our project, and they had approved it. She made it sound like we're doing something illegal. What project could she be doing that ties in with our research? I had a strange feeling other forces were at work here. I thought it best to sit on this for now and not reply immediately.

The summer months turned into fall and the students began to gather for another year. I was busy in the research lab, but for the first time, I only had to worry about my own searches. Deanna was available to me three days a week. She was a teaching assistant for old Dr. Horner in American History 201. This was a sophomore level class that Deanna would have no trouble teaching. Horner had used TAs (Teaching Assistants) to teach this class for years. He had to be in his mid-seventies. I remember his notes for class always being a dingy yellow color from age. It's a good thing history doesn't change.

My first order of business on my own was to set up a schedule. I always operate better with a plan. I began by telling myself that I had to get up every day and do this! To work on your own you need self-discipline.

I made a checklist for all of us to follow. It would make corresponding over the phone or the computer so much easier. The usual information, name, regiment, rank, and enlistment dates, should already be available. Now we needed to establish other variable information, pre-enlistment occupation, marital status, hometown, date of birth if not on file, and hopefully, date of death from national records or county records. Some additional information could be obtained from church records or family diaries. I made check off boxes for each area. I faxed a rough draft to Samantha. She in return faxed me a copy with minor changes. She added a line for date completed and a place to initial who did the research. It was a good working document. Each line of information was numbered for clear reference.

Chapter 4

*"The secret of a good life is to have the right loyalties and
hold them in the right scale of values."*

Norman Thomas

Sussex was a bed of activity in the fall with new students
arriving daily at Oglethorpe. The streets were full of cars.
The local retail stores were booming with business selling
school supplies. Marilyn's Café was a hot spot. The business
of education was good for the local economy. Even Red's
Barber Shop was busy. Pickup trucks with furnishings from
home lined the streets in front of the dormitories.

Oglethorpe came alive after a sleepy summer's rest. The
fall air was refreshing. The leaves on the ancient oak and
sycamore trees tightly grasped the branches, trying to avoid
the inevitable changing of color and then the gentle fall from
grace for another season. This had been the pattern of nature
for countless years.

Samantha had two students help her reorganize Dr. Warren's
office. The college had purchased a new desk for Samantha
and I had authorized the purchase of two file cabinets and
two desktop computers from our grant money. Samantha was
excited about having her own space. The technical support
from our staff at Moss would work out the details to complete
the necessary hookups. I was assured that the programming

and communication links would be up and running within two weeks once work was begun. I figured that everything would be online by September 1. The entire faculty and staff at Oglethorpe were eager to see just how this new project on campus was going to fair. The success, or failure, of the new technology meant a lot to such a small school. It didn't matter what the research involved, that could always be adapted to other disciplines. For now, all eyes were on Dr. Warren and his young assistant, Samantha Martinson.

Samantha began setting up a research plan. She divided the Oglethorpe list into workable segments. She picked six names for her to investigate: Ackley, Alt, Bannon, Bean, Bendalone, and Bergman. Gabe would get Blocker, Caldwell, Carr, Childers, Dix, and Davidson. Samantha listed the names on the checklist sheet as we discussed. The only soldier they had a lead on was Thomas Bean. Samantha had found nothing on him in Ohio County. She planned her next move. The nearest counties in her research area were Jefferson, Ripley, and Dearborn. These three counties would be the most likely to have had an advertisement circulation for Bean Hardware in Aberdeen. It was a logical summation. Samantha had the right idea, divide and conquer, one soldier at a time.

The technical staff was successful in establishing the link between Moss and Oglethorpe. It really only involved the phone lines and setting up designated command codes and ID login names. It was new and exhilarating. Now we were all ready to begin in earnest.

Gabe called Deanna around mid October. We planned on meeting in late November. Gabe set up the meeting at the Ambassador Suite Hotel in Indianapolis. We all agreed on a date, November 21st. It was a race of sorts to see which "team" would have the most results.

Marilyn would also attend the November reunion with Deanna and I. We still had four or five weeks before the meeting. I began checking into the available sites on the Web. I passed a good deal of the site listings on to Gabe and Samantha via e-mail. I couldn't believe the amount of files that were listed.

Whoever decided to use Civil War documents as a test for Internet access made sure they covered all the bases. The official records were printed and made available to the public in 1895, which the average person had probably never seen. The final government investigation and report on the conduct of the war comprised one hundred and twenty-eight bound volumes. The utter quantity of the text was overwhelming. Aside from the sheer magnitude of the records, the reading itself was laborious. These kinds of records and documents are ideal for research, but certainly not easy to get through.

Samantha had decided to start her research with Private Bean. Gabe would start teaching his classes as normal. He would introduce the students to his subject matter and follow a course outline and syllabus. Samantha could dedicate a few days to the project. Gabe would not need her to help with classes for a week or two.

Samantha placed a call to the county clerk in Versailles, the Ripley county seat. Versailles was only eight miles or so north of Sussex. It was the closest of the three counties to Switzerland. Her call was directed to the clerk of the county records office. She explained what her research project involved, and found the records clerk to be extremely willing to take the time to look into Samantha's requests. The easiest way to start was to ask the clerk if there were any records mentioning a Thomas Bean. The area of search would most likely be from 1870 to 1920. They could be tax records, birth records, death records, anything. Of course Samantha knew it would take time to find any information. While she was on the phone, she gave the clerk the names of the other soldiers on her list: Robert Ackley, Ben Alt, James Bannon, Jacob Bendalone, and William Bergman. Maybe she would get lucky. Samantha asked the clerk if they had an e-mail address. The clerk said yes and that she would send the information back by e-mail or fax. Samantha exchanged e-mail addresses and fax numbers with the clerk. Now she would sit back and wait for a reply.

The same procedure was followed for Jefferson County and Dearborn County. Samantha was on a roll. She felt confident that things were off to a great start. This is too easy!

Four days had passed since Samantha made her calls. Her initial joy was beginning to fade. The realization that this was not going to be a simple endeavor began to set in. She had been so sure that she was on the right track, especially with Thomas Bean.

At 4 o'clock in the afternoon of the fifth day, Tuesday, Samantha heard the chirping of a message coming across the fax machine as she stuck her office key in the door lock. Routinely, she opened the door and turned on the light. As she went to hang her jacket on the coatrack, something caught her eye. There were papers in the paper tray of the fax machine. The message included three pages. It was from Donna Mattie, County Records Clerk of Dearborn County. A reply! Samantha stopped dead in her tracks. Could this be what she hoped it would be? Gently she reached down and picked up the three pages. Samantha read the message slowly and with much intensity. The text of the message would be a welcome sight for Gabe. The message read:

Name: Ben Alt, farmer
Married: Betty Welton on 3/21/1872 in Bright, Indiana
Children: Robert 5/11/1873, Judith 12/23/1875, Charles
         9/3/1877
Homestead Tax: 288 acres north of Bright
Death: Charles 8/23/1878
Removed from tax base: 7/7/1881 (Nebraska)
No forwarding address for Ben Alt or Betty Alt
Welton family (in-laws) resided in Bright and Aurora area, still farming.

You may want to contact the Welton side of family for history. One household located in Aurora. Philip Welton, grandson of Robert. 1735 N. Lily Street, Aurora.

If there is anything else I can do for you, let me know.
No information on the other names you mentioned. Hope this helps you.

Donna Mattie, Records, Dearborn County

Samantha burst into joyous laughter. "Yes! Yes! Yes!" She yelled to the four walls of the office. Gabe would be finished with his last class in a matter of minutes. Samantha couldn't wait to show him the fax. It wasn't a find, but it was something firm to go on. Samantha now knew that she had to contact Philip Welton in Aurora. That would be her next move. Gabe would be thrilled.

I sat at my desk staring into the monochrome computer screen. It seemed like I had been here for hours and hours. The phone rang from across the room. Deanna was just coming in the door near the phone. "Hello, Dr. Carls' office, Deanna speaking."

"Deanna, this is Samantha, how are you?" Her voice was clear and full of excitement as she continued. "Deanna, I have a great lead on Ben Alt. I got a bunch of information from the Dearborn County records clerk. Her name is Donna Mattie and she's great. I've got the names of his wife, kids, dates, I got it all. According to Donna, the Alt's moved to Nebraska in 1881."

Deanna's response was typical, a scream of excitement. "Great, good for you. I bet you can't wait to go to Nebraska?"

Samantha reeled back from the phone for a second and then remarked, "Nebraska, I'm not going to Nebraska." She continued, "I hope I can get information from the state archives or somewhere without making a trip. I have another lead on his family. I guess there's a relative living in Aurora,

Indiana, in Dearborn County. I'll probably make a trip there though. That's not very far, about twenty miles from here." "Samantha, that's just wonderful. We may have something going on here as well, but nothing firm. Mr. Carls keeps plugging away every day." Deanna paused and asked, "How's school going? I bet you're pretty tied up with work. If you get any free time, why don't we get together away from the office? You know, a girls' weekend maybe."

Samantha barely had time to comprehend what Deanna had said. Her mind was on the information she had shared. Taken off guard, she said, "Sure, let's do that some time. I'll see you in Indy next month. Let's plan something then."

As soon as Deanna got off the phone, she explained to me what Samantha had found. I was very pleased. Samantha was a go-getter. I knew she'd follow whatever lead she had until it either panned out or disappeared.

Things were starting to happen. All of us rose to a new level of curiosity. It may take awhile, but I for one was sure we could locate all twenty-three soldiers. It would be frustrating at times and hopefully rewarding in the end, but it would be done.

Samantha waited patiently for Gabe to come back to the office. He seemed unusually late. Samantha was to meet a friend at Marilyn's Café at 5 o'clock. She left a note on Gabe's desk telling him to call her later that evening or stop by Marilyn's if he had a chance. Her note finished with a circled "IMPORTANT" at the bottom.

Gabe came in the office at 5:20. His meeting with a new student had run longer than planned. He immediately saw Samantha's note on his desk and without any further thought, he hurried to his car and to Marilyn's. What on earth could be so important?

Samantha sat with her friend Nancy at a table next to the front window. They shared a large order of french fries and were chatting about the new students on campus. Samantha didn't see Gabe come in the door.

Suddenly, Gabe was at the table. He asked Samantha in a panicky voice, "What's wrong?" Gabe's voice was naturally high pitched, but even more so when he was excited.

Samantha was stunned to see him standing there. "Oh," she cried out as she literally jumped up in her seat, "I just wanted to tell you what I found out about Ben Alt today." She reached into her purse and retrieved the fax message.

Gabe took a deep breath, relieved as he sat down in the chair between the two girls. "Samantha, you scared the living hell out of me. I couldn't imagine what was wrong. Your note sounded like we were all fired or something. Please don't do that again, I always think the worst."

"Now, let me see what you found out today about old Ben." Gabe read Donna's notes carefully. "So, Sam, when are you going to Aurora?" Gabe was very pleased with Samantha's success. She had great initiative. As they shared their excitement with Nancy, Gabe asked if maybe he could do some research on one or two soldiers, or whether Samantha was going do it all. Of course he was joking. He would get his chance very soon.

The end of the week came rather quickly. Gabe thought, as all teachers do: *Another week gone.* He wondered if he had covered the material in class as well as he had planned. Sometimes the best made plans fall through. He sat at his desk jotting down notes to himself when the ringing of the phone broke the silence in the office. It was Gene Fife from Vevay.

"Hello, this Dr. Warren?" Gene half-shouted in the phone with his southern drawl.

"Yes," responded Gabe. "Who is this?"

"I'm Gene Fife. I work in county records over here in Vevay. I worked with Mike Carls last winter. He gave me your number and told me to call you if anything came up about those fellas you're all looking for. Well, something has all right. Some lady named Krista Butler called here asking questions about your research. I didn't like the way she sounded. I told her Mike was here, but I didn't tell her any more than that. Wonder what she's snooping for?"

Gabe was taking notes as Gene talked. He remembered me telling him about Gene and Dorothy Fife. Good people. "Mr. Fife," Gabe replied, "I'm glad you called me. I'll call Mr. Carls immediately. I don't know who this Krista person is, but I'll pass your concerns on to him. He'll probably call you back. Are you at home or in your office?"

Gene chuckled and said, "I'm at work, it ain't no office. Mike knows both my numbers. Have him call me at the house later tonight. I just thought you folks needed to know about this here woman right away."

Gabe thanked Gene and promised to keep in touch with him. Gabe's call to me came just as I was about to leave the office for the day. His voice sounded worried. I told him about my contact with Miss Butler, but I couldn't imagine why she would bother Gene. For some reason, this woman was monitoring our progress. Why? Gabe and I discussed the situation. Neither of us had a clue why this Krista would be so interested in our work. I had put her out of my mind after her e-mail to me. Now I had to find out who she was and what she wanted. I called Gene and thanked him for not sharing any detailed information. I also told him I had no idea who she was or what she wanted. Gene agreed to call Gabe or me if Miss Butler contacted him again.

I turned my computer back on and went to my e-mail file that brought up Krista's original message. I tried to analyze what was in front of me. First of all, how did she get my e-mail address? Secondly, what did she mean by she's only interested in "who" was doing the research on Civil War soldiers? She also mentioned a "mutual" organization. It had to be the National Science Commission. Who else could it be? I put this off to the side before, now I had to ask questions. I would contact the NSC first thing Monday morning.

Chapter 5

"It is dangerous to be right when the government is wrong."

Voltaire

The Washington operator gave me the number for the National Science Commission, 713-241-3471. I asked her to connect me if she could. She then asked what department I wanted. I told her I was looking for Krista Butler in computer development. She put me on hold for a brief second while she checked the extension. I was grasping for information and playing on an assumption. I was dumbfounded when she came back on the line and told me that Miss Butler was currently working in the computer development area as well as in the biological and human health department.

"Which of Miss Butler's extensions would you like me to connect you with, sir?"

I thought for a second and then answered somewhat hesitantly, "Computer development."

The phone rang twice before a young female voice answered, "Computers, Krista speaking."

Again I hesitated. "Krista Butler? This is Michael Carls from Moss University. I believe we have something to talk about?"

Krista responded quickly, "Yes, Mr. Carls, are you in Illinois or are you in Washington?"

"I'm in Illinois."

Krista fumbled for words. "I suppose you have some questions for me?"

I hadn't planned on actually talking to Krista in detail at this time, but the time was now. I came straight out and asked her, "What interest do you have in my research, and why would you bother someone that I spoke to last winter? And another thing, how did you get my e-mail address?"

"Mr. Carls, I assure you I meant no harm to Mr. Fife in Vevay. I am doing a computer project that tracks Internet users. It may seem like an invasion of privacy, but it's just a way for us here at NSC to see how the Internet is being used. You can understand that, can't you?"

I wasn't quite sure how to respond. She made it sound so innocent and practicable. I asked her, "Is that what you meant when you said you were only interested in *who* was doing the research?"

"Exactly," was her immediate reply, "I meant no harm. I was in Cincinnati and thought I would stop in to see Mr. Fife in Vevay since I was so close. Again, I have no additional interest in your work." I was satisfied with her explanation.

I told Krista I would let her know if I needed to venture into new areas of documentation. Perhaps the NSC could help me at the same time I would be helping them develop an easier access route for future users. I said good-bye to Miss Butler.

As I sat there rethinking our conversation, it occurred to me that I should have asked her how she knew about Gene Fife? I hadn't e-mailed him or had any computer contact with him. I don't even think he had a computer when I was there. She got me on that one. I should have asked her how they track computer users. The system had been used by the military for years before any civilian knew about it. I have always been suspicious about what the government or the military can listen in on or track, especially with all the new satellite technology in recent years.

For now I'd settle for Miss Butler's explanation. I had work to do. Others were depending on me to be the team leader. I waited for Deanna to finish her class for Dr. Horner. It wouldn't be long. I walked over to David Hinman's work area. He was sitting back reading a *Sports Illustrated* magazine, his feet propped up on his desk. I guess I surprised him; he damn near fell over backwards when I came around the corner. "Dr. Carls, I wasn't expecting you!" I just laughed, "Of course you weren't. You were expecting Dr. Darling, right?"

David was doing a project on East African tribal customs. It was something that normally I would be doing. It really was quite interesting. I was always amazed at how different we can all be on this earth. Why is it that some countries develop and others never seem to? It doesn't seem right. David had charts and notes pinned up all over his cubicle walls. He was enjoying his brief tenure so far.

We engaged in a lively conversation on the life expectancy of African tribes. David had taken United Nations records and compiled a chart based on age and death records. Again, I found these facts disturbing. Tribes in eastern African nations had almost no infant mortalities, yet tribes in the west had figures as high as 40 percent! Why?

The life expectancy rates were just as startling. In some tribes, age forty-five was considered old. In other tribes, there were recorded ages of 110 or 120 years. What could account for such wide variations? David was into his work. He explained this and that about his research and how he came up with his information. As I listened, I began to think, *How could our teams use the same method here in the States to find death records for all Civil War veterans? Was it even possible?*

Deanna came in, the lab and collapsed at her desk. "Man, am I tired. I don't think I can put up with these students for a whole year."

I smiled and watched her. "Deanna, it's your chosen field, your passion, you know you love it, and you only have thirty more years before you can retire. Isn't it fun?"

Deanna rolled her head on her folded arms as she lay on the desk and looked at me. "Are you kidding," she continued, "I'm marrying some rich hunk and staying home to raise my two perfect kids in my perfect little home." We both got a chuckle out of that.

When I got back to work, I searched the Internet for death records on a per state basis. There wasn't much to find. Some states had set up websites, but even then only a few counties were listed. I would have to look elsewhere or physically go to each county. I knew that wouldn't be possible. Deanna buried herself in papers from her students. She had her students write essay responses to twenty questions. It would take a great deal of time to read them all.

At 2 o'clock Deanna broke away from reading. I thought this would be a good time to share my discussion with her about Miss Butler. Deanna asked if I wanted a Coke from the vending machine down the hall.

"Sure, I'll buy."

When she returned, we went to the lounge at the end of the hall. Luckily, no one else was there. We each took a sofa and got comfortable.

"Well, what did Miss Butler have to say?" Deanna asked.

I went on to tell her about the NSC's monitoring of Internet use and that they were not interested in our research, but only in what sites we were using or not using.

I could see from her expression that Deanna wasn't buying it. "That's a bunch of BS. They're up to something. What did she say about visiting Gene in Vevay?"

I was embarrassed to tell her that I fell for the story about being so close in Cincinnati.

Deanna had a good feel for people and she was quick to analyze situations. "We better keep an eye on Miss Butler. I don't think she's telling us everything up-front. I smell trouble. It just doesn't feel right."

I had to admit, Deanna had a point. There had to be more to Miss Butler's interest than Internet users. I was especially concerned about how she knew about my trip to Vevay and Gene Fife. That was worrisome.

I tried to focus on my research. Trying to keep everything straight and on track was a full-time job. I didn't have time to worry about the NSC or Krista Butler. I'd face that challenge when it arose again.

The cursor on my computer screen kept flashing at me, as if asking, "What should I do next?" I couldn't concentrate. Thoughts of Miss Butler and the NSC lingered in my head. I thought to myself, *Let's look into the mission of the NSC. It's a government agency; there must be some public information available.* I did a computer search, nothing.

It was only a short walk to the campus library. I hadn't been inside there since my meeting with Wes last winter. Nancy Longan was the head librarian. She had helped me thousands of times over the years. Nancy was more than just dedicated to her profession. She was a wealth of information. If there was a shortcut to find something, she knew how to take it.

Nancy directed me to the reference section of the library and on to a rather portentous-looking text. The title alone was a mouthful: *The Official Listing of United States of America Governmental Agencies, Bureaus, Sub-Agencies, Commissions, and Councils.* I made myself comfortable at one of Nancy's lovely oak tables. I knew I'd be camped here for a while.

On page 162, under Bureaus and Commissions, I found the Congressional document establishing the National Science Commission. The NSC was headed up by its own Inspector General, appointed by the president. The Commission had begun operation in 1950. The main disciplines of the NSC were the studies of biology, education, technical advancement, and health. What I found particularly interesting was a small ending statement in the original document. It stated that the mission of the Commission was to " . . . progress science and advance the national health." I wondered what it meant by *advance the national health?* Whatever it meant, they had a budget of $3.5 billion dollars to do it. Now I understood how I received our grant request and more.

I was satisfied for the time being; best get back to work. It was raining lightly as I walked back to my office. I was just about to focus my afternoon on Private Overland when Dave Hinman stuck his head around the corner of my cubicle. Catching my glance, he said, "I think I found something you may find interesting. The web page guys in D.C. just downloaded more Civil War files. You've heard of the G.A.R., the Grand Army of the Republic, right? Well, these records from are from1890 to 1956. Perhaps some of the names you're looking for are included." I followed Dave's lead and opened up GrandArmyoftheRepublic.org.

Dave was right, there were tens of thousands of names listed by state, regiment, and rank, and some included obituaries. This could be the break we were looking for. I could think of no other source that would be this helpful.

The G.A.R. was founded in Decatur, Illinois, on April 6,1866, by Union veteran Dr. Benjamin Franklin Stephenson. The Grand Army had three cardinal principals, Fraternity, Charity, and Loyalty. This was a fraternal organization with over 400,000 members nationwide. In the 1890s they were quite political and commanded a great deal of influence. One of the key features of the G.A.R. was that they sponsored national reunions, known as encampments, every year. These were gatherings of delegates from all G.A.R. posts around the country. Aside from conducting business matters, these encampments became more and more important as a final meeting arena for surviving Civil War veterans as the years passed.

The final encampment of the G.A.R. took place in 1949 at Indianapolis, Indiana. From a peak membership of 409,489 in 1890, only six old soldiers attended the Indianapolis encampment. On the agenda at this final meeting was one order of business, the vote to disband. According to the web page information, the last member of the Grand Army of the Republic died on August 2,1956. His name was Albert Wollson of Duluth, Minnesota. He was 109 years old.

I read the G.A.R. pages with undivided interest. I could almost feel the passing of a legend as the last link to the Civil War disappeared. I was actually saddened by reading these reports. However, I could certainly see that the information contained here would be of great value to our research. I began to scour the files for the names of the soldiers on my list. I saw immediately that it was going to be an arduous task. The membership files for the G.A.R. were not in alphabetical order. They were listed by post, by state. I questioned, *How many posts were there and how could I possibly know what post any of these soldiers might have belonged to?* Deanna and I would have to assume that the local soldiers returned home or somewhere nearby. I always hate to assume anything. I'm usually wrong!

Deanna came into the office on Friday morning and I broke the news to her about the G.A.R. files. She is always upbeat and ready for a challenge so she was eager to get started. We only had one more week before our meeting with Gabe and Samantha in Indianapolis. All of us, Deanna, Marilyn, and I were looking forward to getting together again. Deanna wanted to have something positive in hand to show Samantha. We had a feeling we were on the right track.

Almost immediately Deanna found the name of Daniel Hales. The G.A.R. records listed him as a member in St. Louis, Missouri, in 1904. Deanna followed up her find with a call to the St. Louis county clerk's office in St. Louis. In just a matter of minutes, after explaining what our inquiry was about, she was able to ascertain that Private Hales of Company I, 14th Indiana Infantry had died on December 11, 1907 and is buried in St. Michael's Cemetery in St. Louis. We were both elated and in shock at the same time. The break we were hoping for seemed to be in our hands.

Chapter 6

"I'm a great believer in luck, and I find the harder I work the more I have of it."

Thomas Jefferson

Marilyn was in a buzz, rushing around the house packing for our "weekend away" in Indianapolis. She had asked off of work for Wednesday the 19th through Friday the 21st. She had a million questions for me ranging from "Is there a pool?" to "What are the girls wearing?"

It was a good thing we decided to take Marilyn's Caravan, considering the amount of luggage she was taking. My only salvation was that Deanna was riding down with us and I told Marilyn to leave some room for Deanna's bags. Marilyn had a history of taking everything she owns for overnighters!

I did my faithful hubby thing and called the hotel in Indianapolis. The front-desk clerk at the Ambassador Suites was most helpful in answering my questions and solving all of Marilyn's concerns. Yes, they had an indoor heated pool. They also had a steam room, dry sauna, and two whirlpools. What I didn't tell Marilyn was that we would be only a short walk from the new Union Station Retail Mall. I figured it wouldn't take her and Deanna long to figure out that one. The purpose of this meeting was to compare notes and update each other on what progress we had made. However, we did need time to relax and enjoy each other's company.

Marilyn packed my usual items. I liked to dress casually whenever I could. Late November required sweaters and long-sleeved shirts. Marilyn had packed a number of slacks outfits and one dressy outfit for a night out. Of course the ladies, Deanna and Marilyn, had talked about attire and who was bringing what. They decided one hair dryer would just have to do.

Deanna's last class on Thursday the 20th ended at 3:30. She rushed to our house and we were ready to hit the road by 4:00. I wanted to get an hour's drive out of the way before we stopped for supper.

Luckily, we hadn't had any snow to contend with. The roads were clear. We stopped in Morris, Illinois, fifty-five miles from our start. It felt good to get away, especially for Marilyn; she was almost giddy with joy. I ate while the ladies continued their endless girl talk.

Traffic was reasonably light for a Friday night on the Interstate. The drive from Champaign, Illinois, to the Indiana border was fast. We pulled into Indianapolis at 8:45. The Ambassador Suite Hotel was in the heart of downtown and easy to get to. The only construction we encountered was just a few blocks west of the hotel. A new venue was being built for the upcoming Pan Am Games next summer.

The Ambassador was a beautiful hotel with eighteen floors and 360 two-room suites. Our rooms on the sixteenth floor had a v breathtaking view. To the north was Monument Circle with its bronze statue of *Victory* atop the 230-foot spire on the Soldiers' and Sailors' Monument. The lights of the city to the east were just beautiful.

Marilyn and Deanna were eager to check out the rest of the hotel. The indoor pool was located on the sixth floor and was small, but inviting. The interior lobby was a courtyard. The hotel rooms surrounded the hollow core of the center. Deanna and Samantha had requested to share a room, which was next to Marilyn's and mine.

The three of us were walking in the lounge area when Gabe and Samantha arrived. There were warm greetings all around. Gabe placed their luggage on a bell cart and invited all of us for a drink at the piano bar. It had been a long day already so we gladly accepted his offer. The soothing tone of the piano and the mood within the room was very relaxing. The piano sat in the corner of the room inside solid glass walls. The lounge itself was dark with small cut glass amber candles on each table. The music with the night lights in the background made the whole experience unforgettable. It was late and we had all driven a good distance. Marilyn and I were ready to call it a night and get some sleep. Marilyn wanted to sleep in, so we agreed to meet in the courtyard lobby at 9:00. Gabe, Deanna, and Samantha stayed in the lounge enjoying each other's company for another two hours.

Instead of going right to bed, Marilyn and I decided to take a late-night swim. It was a relaxing way to unwind.

We walked into the main-floor lounge area at 8:45. Gabe was already on his second cup of coffee and had ordered breakfast. Marilyn and I joined him. I assumed the girls would be down a bit later.

I asked Gabe if his room was also on the sixteenth floor. He said, "No, they moved me down a couple of floors to room 1211, something about a group down the hall from you folks needing an extra room. I didn't mind the move."

I always like these kinds of hotels where you can order ala cart, or something special from the chef. Marilyn had the best Denver Omelet ever! It was 9:10 when Deanna and Samantha joined us. They looked like they had been up all night talking. Samantha, who never drinks coffee, ordered a cup of black coffee immediately. Deanna just had her normal orange juice.

Our meeting got underway at 10:30. We camped out at a large round table in the main-floor lounge. The overstuffed chairs were comfy. We spread out papers everywhere.

Deanna started things out by presenting her material on Daniel Hales and the G.A.R. Gabe and Samantha were vigorously taking notes. The new G.A.R. website was going to be very helpful in our research.

Things were happening fast in the computer field as new websites were being added daily. There would probably be more sites up and running by the time we got home. Gabe and Samantha were both feeling an increased comfort level with their new computers. They were still toying with various websites, but that was the fun of it: explore and see what you can find. The faculty members at Oglethorpe were quite interested in their work. Gabe's office was the only place on campus where the Internet could be accessed. Gabe had several articles from professional journals indicating that the general public would have Internet capabilities within a year or two.

After exchanging notes and concerns about the G.A.R. website and its potential impact on our research, we all needed a break. Marilyn suggested that all four of us take a scenic walk to Monument Circle. It was only two blocks north of the hotel. The Soldiers' and Sailors' Monument was impressive. We visited Christ Church Cathedral, the ceremonial seat of the Bishop of Indianapolis. The church was built in 1857 and had beautiful Tiffany stained-glass windows. When visiting the area, it's a must-see!

We really enjoyed the afternoon. Marilyn seemed to notice something in the air about Gabe and Samantha. I have to admit, I thought I saw them looking at each other a little flirtatiously. Could it be that they have become "an item"?

Gabe and I watched as Marilyn, Deanna, and Samantha took the elevator to the observation deck of the monument. I wasn't one for small cramped high places. We couldn't pass up the unique gift shops on the square. Gabe had picked the most ideal spot for our meeting.

As the ladies shopped at Union Station Retail Mall, Gabe and I trailed behind and talked about our careers and the various things we had each accomplished in our fields. We were really getting to know one another quite well. At one point our discussion turned to Gabe's working relationship with Samantha. He told me that Samantha had been his assistant for nearly eighteen months now. Gabe also volunteered that he and Samantha had actually dated just recently. He said that they were not serious at this point and that the powers to be at Oglethorpe would frown on any such relationship. He wanted to make Marilyn and I aware of the situation, but they were keeping things under wraps in Sussex. Gabe assured me that none of this would interfere in any way with the project. I was pleased with his honest and forthright approach. I respected that.

While we were in the downtown area, we walked over to the state archives, just three blocks off the square. As tourists, and not researchers, we asked to talk to an archivist about the Civil War. We were introduced to a nice young man named Franklin Jones. Mr. Jones, about thirty years old, was more than accommodating of our inquiries.

The five of us followed him downstairs to a room filled with microfiche viewing machines. Franklin showed us how a client could order information from an archivist and privately view virtually any film they had on file. Deanna, Samantha, and Marilyn had never seen microfiche material before. Again, the volume of records available was enormous. No one could possibly look at all this material. If we planned on using this method of research, we would have to be very precise. Before leaving the archives, Gabe and I made plans to meet with Franklin the next day. Franklin had told us that they would be open from 8:00 a.m. to noon on Saturday.

We had dinner at St. Elmo's Steakhouse on Illinois Street. Our steaks were exquisite. They had a 20,000-bottle wine cellar with some of the best Cabernets and Bordeaux's I've ever seen. The atmosphere of the restaurant was most distinctive. The evening was great. Good food, good conversation, good friends. Gabe and I talked business as well as sports and politics. We covered the whole spectrum. Marilyn was having the time of her life with Deanna and Samantha. She was very relaxed and enjoying her Kahlúa and Creams.

It was nearly 2:00 before we returned to the Ambassador. The ladies were looking forward to sleeping in late in the morning. Gabe and I were going to try and be at the archives as early as possible.

We met Franklin at the archives shortly after 9:00 and seemed to have the building all to ourselves. Franklin directed us to a thick index that resembled a Chicago phonebook. It must have been four inches thick.

Microfiche films contained records of everything imaginable—complete newspapers, death certificates, birth certificates, magazine articles, service records, pension records, and more.

Gabe thought immediately of looking for information on the G.A.R. He found index listings for all local G.A.R. posts, a major find. There were 598 posts in Indiana located in virtually every city and town in the 1890s. If any of our soldiers had been a G.A.R. member in the state, we should find their names. Scouring each post's roster could take months. Gabe threw himself wholeheartedly into the task. Although we had the names of all the soldiers with us, there was no need to refer to our briefcases. Their names were imbedded in our memories.

I searched under the heading of Military Discharges. I found nothing. Our soldiers were not listed. I found this peculiar since Hales and Alt had survived the war and apparently lived for a number of years. Strange. I guess it could have been an oversight, but why? And what about pensions? Surely these men would have wanted to collect their pensions. I suppose every system hadd its glitches. It just struck me as odd that two men from the same regiment could be discharged without any record.

Gabe and I were working the machines slowly, browsing each page carefully. On the other hand, Franklin was zipping through pages of information. We told him what we were interested in finding. He had a keen eye. Franklin had a way of bypassing the fringe and getting right to the heart of the matter.

By 11:45 we had a mountain of facts and figures. To say that Lady Luck was on our side today would be putting it mildly. Franklin made copies of everything for us and we exchanged phone and fax numbers. He was genuinely interested in our research and especially interested in the Internet system for the future. Gabe gave Franklin a list of our soldiers and Franklin said he would continue to look for additional material that would be of help. Our morning had been most productive.

As we walked into the hotel, Samantha and Marilyn were in the main lounge area eating a late breakfast. We walked over and laid our armful of sixty-four copies on their table.

"So, what you guy's been up to this morning?" Marilyn mused.

"Well," replied Gabe, "just watching a little black-and-white screen for the last three hours. And what time did you princesses roll out of bed?"

Marilyn laughed and said, "Oh, sometime after you left." That was a safe answer. Who cares; they rested and we found a ton of material.

After joining Samantha and Marilyn for coffee, I strolled upstairs to get something from my room. As I passed Deanna's door, I knocked to see if she was awake. It was already past noon. Deanna came to the door looking quite unlike herself. I said, "Good morning, it's lunchtime."

Deanna just ran her hands through her hair and walked back into the room. "Give me a few minutes," she mumbled as she yawned deeply. "I think those Black Russians attacked me last night." Deanna did not drink very often. Black Russians go down easy but catch up to you later.

After lunch we met again in the main lounge. Gabe began spreading out the papers from the archives on the large round mahogany coffee table in the middle of the lounge. Samantha sighed: just imagining the work ahead. Deanna sat emotionless until Gabe brought up the numbers involved. Our first plan of attack was to search the G.A.R. post listing. We would have to search the hard copies in front of us and then try to match them with files on the websites.

Gabe began by explaining, "Indiana at one time, in the 1890s, had 598 G.A.R. posts. A post is equivalent to today's American Legion or V.F.W. If we assume that each post had between twenty and fifty members, the number of names could be from 12,000 to 30,000, and that's just Indiana. If any of our soldiers moved to others states, we could be scouring through one to two million names. I think we need to limit our area of search and hope for the best. It's highly possible that, although we have had some success, we never find several of these men."

The magnitude of Gabe's assessment was apparent on everyone's face. Gabe continued, "Neighboring states like Illinois and Kentucky, had 772 posts and 219 posts, respectively. The numbers just become mind-boggling. Mike and I have talked and we think we can manage this angle of research if we divide the posts into clusters and go from there."

"Since the 14th Indiana was mustered in at Terre Haute, let's concentrate on a four or five county area surrounding the city. That is one cluster. We should also assume that some of these men might have moved to west-central Illinois after the war to farm or seek other employment. That's another cluster and one that may include ten or twelve eastern Illinois counties. We already know that a few of these guys lived in our area in southern Indiana and possibly northern Kentucky. In that case, we should look to the counties surrounding Louisville, Kentucky. We'll continue our search in the Sussex area. Do you agree on any of this or does someone else have a better idea?"

Samantha was the first to speak. "Gabe . . . I mean Dr. Warren . . . I'd like to continue in the four counties I'm already in contact with back home, but I would also like to take on the Louisville area as well. Do you think that's doable?"

Marilyn sat forward in her chair and laughed as she said, "Samantha honey, I think we can allow you to call Dr. Warren by his first name. None of us are blind here. I think you two make a nice couple. You don't need to hide behind the closet doors with us." We all got a laugh out of that and I just smiled at Gabe. Gabe was a bit embarrassed, but it was best to get things out on the table. Deanna leaned over and hugged Samantha. The girls had been talking!

With that out of the way, we assigned areas to research. Even Marilyn wanted some work to do. I was very proud of her. She was really getting into it. Marilyn and Deanna would come up with a list of counties in Illinois. I had the time to travel, so I took on Terre Haute and the surrounding counties. Gabe had his teaching assignment and probably the least amount of free time. He would help Samantha. I suggested that we make an offer to Gene Fife in Vevay to assist us. We could offer him some amount of money for his time and travel. Samantha could certainly use the help. Everyone agreed that with his background and familiarity with the area, Gene would be a good addition to our team. Gabe would contact Gene when they returned to Oglethorpe.

Gabe and I passed out the lists of all the G.A.R. posts for each of the states, Indiana, Illinois, and Kentucky. On each list were the locations and the name of each post. For instance, the post in Terre Haute, in Vigo County, is named the Oliver P. Morton Post. Marilyn and Deanna's eyes nearly popped out of their heads when they saw their list. Seven hundred and seventy-two post's, wow!

The hard copy lists for Indiana and Kentucky broke the post locations down by county and city. The Illinois list mentioned the county, but instead was organized by the post's name and city. The Illinois search would more difficult to manage. Marilyn and Deanna studied their list. Marilyn excused herself for a minute and went to our van to retrieve a Rand McNally Atlas and a State of Indiana road map.

Samantha unfolded the Indiana map on the carpet in front of her chair. I joined her, sitting Indian fashion, on the floor. We began highlighting the names of counties surrounding Terre Haute. Our list included Vigo, Putnam, Parks, Fountain, and Vermillion. We thought this was a logical starting point. I would now go over my list of posts within each county and circle each city on the map. I had no idea how many posts might had be located in this five county area. It could be several dozen.

Meanwhile, Deanna and Marilyn were circling the names of cities and towns in east-central Illinois. It was a random guessing game. They also decided to add Cook County, mainly Chicago, to their search. After the war, soldiers may have relocated there because of the availability of employment.

Gabe was busy writing down the names of the counties he and Samantha already had contact with. When Deanna and Marilyn finished with the atlas, they passed it to Gabe and Samantha. Samantha was familiar with the Louisville area. The two of them wrote down the names of five counties: Bullit, Campbell, Jefferson, Kenton, and Meade. All of these counties bordered Indiana and were relatively close to Sussex in case a visit was needed.

We spent the remainder of the afternoon making lists and exchanging copies of each cluster with one another. We appreciated the hotel staff letting us use their copy machine.

Now each of us had a full set of search areas in case we needed to fill in for each other for some unforeseen reason.

At 4 o'clock we broke up our meeting and had a round of well-deserved drinks—on me. We couldn't believe how far our project had advanced and yet how much more there was to do. Gabe was particularly impressed by everyone's enthusiasm and dedication. We were in it for the long haul. We were committed to finding as many of these men as humanly possible. For now, we put away our papers and maps and prepared to enjoy our last night together in Indianapolis.

Marilyn and I were the first ones down from our room and waited in the piano bar for the others. Gabe came in shortly after we sat down. Marilyn had planned the evening's activities. She was so good at doing these kinds of things. She loved to entertain and had a great sense for detail.

Samantha and Deanna arrived in the bar within ten minutes. The ladies looked simply beautiful. Marilyn must have called and told the girls to bring some formalwear. Marilyn wore a stunning black sequined dress. Deanna's dress was royal blue and nearly floor length. Samantha cut quite a pose with a red floor-length dress slit up one side. Her black hair and eyes made the perfect match. They were all lovely. Gabe and I had on two-piece dark suits. Marilyn said this would be a night on the town. She wasn't wrong.

We enjoyed an intimate dinner in a small European-style restaurant on Talbott Street, just east of Monument Circle. The charbroiled steaks and steamed vegetables were scrumptious. For dessert we indulged in chocolate mousse; again, good times and great food. After dinner we returned to the Ambassador and the adjoining Indiana Repertory Theatre. Although Marilyn and I had seen *The Mouse That Roared* performed on our campus at home, the production here was equally as entertaining.

We ended our evening back in the hotel piano bar. We had shared two unforgettable days. All of us were wiser for them. We all retired shortly after midnight. The morning would come soon enough and then the long drive home. The holidays were fast approaching. Although we wouldn't be together for Thanksgiving, we were certainly thankful for our time together in Indianapolis. We made plans to get together again in the spring. It was my turn to determine the time and place. It would be hard to top our experience here in Indiana.

Deanna had made arrangements with Dr. Horner to have her classes covered for the next two weeks. She would go with Gabe and Samantha and visit Sussex and become better acquainted with their research. Marilyn and I would take a slow trip home.

After breakfast we all packed our belongings and said our good-byes. It was about 9:30 when we left Indianapolis. I would meet Samantha and Deanna in Terre Haute in a couple of weeks when Deanna and I would begin our county investigations there.

Chapter 7

"Minds are like parachutes; they work best when open."

Lord Thomas Dewar

Sunday morning was always a great day for a drive in southern Indiana. Traffic was nearly nonexistent. And today the weather was perfect, not a cloud in the sky.

Gabe drove along as the girls talked and joked around. Deanna was sprawled out on the backseat. She was comfortable. Samantha sat half turned around, talking. Samantha was planning their time together and asked Deanna if she had ever been to Louisville.

Deanna said, "Yes, but it has been a long time." Samantha knew some great nightlife places.

"Well," said Samantha, "Gabe and I'll take you down next weekend. You'll love it. We have some favorite spots to show you."

Deanna couldn't help but notice how beautiful the countryside was. The rolling grassy hills and vineyards were a far cry from northern Illinois. Samantha commented on the trees, regaling their beauty in the fall. As for the vineyards, there were plenty of local wineries.

By noon, Gabe was pulling into Sussex. Deanna gazed out the window expectantly. "I've heard so much about Sussex from Mr. Carls. He just loved it down here. Now I know why." Deanna was enjoying her retreat.

Gabe parked the car alongside Farbeck Hall. "Come on Deanna, we'll show you the office first." The air was chilly, yet refreshing. The last of the autumn leaves were lying in the campus square. The only sound was the crunching of the leaves underfoot. The students were either in their rooms or gone for the weekend. Deanna thought the campus was charming.

Samantha and Deanna ran ahead of Gabe, who had his briefcase in hand. Samantha unlocked the door to Draper Hall and led Deanna down the stairs. "This is it," Samantha announced.

Deanna looked around. "Cozy," she replied.

Gabe came down the stairs and entered the office saying, "It's smaller than you're used to, but it serves its purpose."

"Oh no, Gabe, I think it's great. How much room do you really need anyway?"

After dropping off a few things at the office, Samantha suggested they go to Marilyn's for lunch. Deanna was looking forward to meeting this Marilyn. "I assure you, Deanna, our Marilyn isn't anything like your Marilyn," Gabe blurted. Samantha couldn't hold back a laugh.

Deanna sat quietly waiting for Marilyn to appear. Instead, a thirtyish waitress named Amanda came to the table. Marilyn wasn't working. Even without Marilyn there, lunch was fine. Deanna would have to wait another day.

After lunch the threesome strolled greater downtown Sussex. It wasn't a very long walk. Deanna liked the small-town atmosphere. As they headed back to Gabe's car, Samantha veered to the left while holding Deanna's arm. "I live just around the corner. You're staying with me. Besides, I have never had a guest in my apartment. You're the first. I just moved out of the dorm this past September. I love being alone." Deanna understood. She had had her own apartment for nearly two years.

Gabe pulled the car around the corner and parked out front. Samantha lived on the second floor of an old Victorian house of Scandinavian origin. The outside of the old home was covered in ornamental flair. The house had four different colors of paint. Samantha pointed out that it was called a "Painted Lady." The house dated back to the 1870s. The rooms were large by today's standards. It had a single bath with a claw-footed bathtub. Samantha had it decorated with contemporary '80s flair.

Gabe carried in the luggage for both girls. "Thanks for the help guys," Gabe sighed. "I just love your stairs, Samantha." Samantha tipped her head in recognition; she was too busy showing Deanna around. It only took Gabe a second to land on the sofa. He was ready for a nap.

After unpacking again, Deanna decided to rest as well. Samantha was in the kitchen trying to create something for dinner later. It had been a long weekend.

Deanna slept in until 10:00 Monday morning. Samantha had been at school for two hours. Deanna rose, dressed, and walked to Marilyn's for breakfast. Finally, she met Marilyn.

"Good morning, young lady," greeted Marilyn. "You must be Deanna. Samantha was in earlier. She said you'd be in for breakfast. Glad to meet you. I met your boss last winter when he was here." Deanna wasn't quite fully awake yet.

"Nice to meet you, too, Marilyn. Could I get a large OJ, please?"

"Sure, honey," Marilyn, said as she dashed off to place another order at the grill. When she returned, she asked if

Deanna wanted breakfast. "No, ma'am, I don't usually do more than orange juice."

Deanna walked the three blocks to Draper Hall. Early morning walks were one of Deanna's favorites when she got the chance to get out. Gabe was in class and Samantha was not in the office. From across the hall, Samantha could see Deanna looking for someone.

"Over here, Deanna."

Deanna followed the sound of Samantha's voice. "What are you doing down there?"

Samantha looked around a file cabinet. "Oh, I have a stack of files back here in one of these boxes. They painted our office over the summer and we had to clear everything out of their way. I hope I can find all the files. What a mess."

Deanna wanted to help. "Can I move something for you?" Deanna offered. The two girls moved several pieces of office furniture and file cabinets that hadn't made it back to their respective offices.

Finally, Samantha found the research files she had been looking for. "Great," she exclaimed, "They're dumped all over the floor back here. What a bunch of morons. We'll waste half the day sorting out all this stuff."

They spread the papers and notes out on the floor. Samantha tried to remember what went where. Luckily, the files were labeled correctly. There were nearly eighty file folders to fill. I had taken fifteen from Samantha last winter.

It's funny how when you put something back together you find things that may have been overlooked the first time. Samantha did just that. As she sifted through the papers, she ran across the names of Bergman and Carr. She knew she had missed this before. Perhaps something in these files could help her now. She handed this particular file to Deanna and told her to hang on to it. With so many files stored away, it was easy to see how things could get overlooked.

Samantha was noticeably upset with herself. "Damn, I don't know what's wrong with me. I should know what to look for. I'm supposed to be a researcher. I don't know if we'll ever going to make sense of this; and for what? Who really cares if we find these guys? They're all dead and gone anyway. Big deal, the NSC wants to know if their Internet thing works or not."

Deanna let out a deep sigh. "Samantha," she said, "look at it this way: It's not about finding all these soldiers, it's about the system. Can it work for future research? If information is shared between people, governments, schools, hospitals, doctors, scientists, look how good that can be. That's what we're doing. No one really cares about some old soldiers. They're the means to an end. We're creating that end; we're testing the system. That's why we have to go on and do this. Don't give up. It's frustrating, of course, but look at the benefits if we succeed."

Samantha nodded. She knew Deanna was right. This project was bigger than them. She handed Deanna another folder and they continued to fill files for the remainder of the afternoon.

Deanna and Samantha stayed up late talking about growing up and family and the guys they had dated. On Tuesday morning I called Gabe's office to give Deanna some additional information. She was going to try to get over to Vevay and meet Gene Fife. I could tell from the sound of her voice that she wasn't quite awake yet. She said she was having a great time.

I asked her if she could follow up on Corporal Hayes for me. I gave her the name of the Methodist church in Moorefield. It was only a short distance from Sussex. Maybe she could find something there.

Deanna then posed a strange question. "Mr. Carls," she asked, "I know we've located some of these guys here as well as from our office, but how can there be no records of discharges or pensions? That just seems so strange to me. Am I missing something, or are the records just full of holes?" I thought about her questions for a moment before responding.

"Deanna," I said, "I don't know why the records are incomplete. All we can do is continue to eliminate the names of the missing and bring closure to those files. I think we're off to a good start. Keep working the angles we have been and let's see where it leads us. You just have a good time and relax. Work with Gabe and Samantha on the soldiers we've identified in that area. Let me know before you head for Terre Haute. I'll make reservations there ahead of time and I'll talk to you then, okay?"

"You're right as usual. We'll get busy. Samantha and I are planning to go to Aurora today and see Ben Alt's family. I'll call you later this week. Bye for now."

It sounded like the girls had a plan. That's good. Their trip should take care of one more name on our list. I had my own list to work on.

Deanna was still in awe of the countryside. Samantha's little Beetle hugged the road. The terrain heading toward Aurora was very hilly. Samantha had made arrangements to meet with Robert Welton, great-great-grandson of Ben Alt, at the Oak Leaf Restaurant for lunch. The restaurant was just outside of Aurora.

As they pulled into the parking lot, a tall man in his mid-forties got out of a blue Ford F-150 pickup truck and waved at Samantha's car. Samantha had told him what kind of car she would be driving.

"Howdy, I'm Bob Welton," he greeted them.

Samantha was the first one out of the car. "Hi, I'm Samantha Martinson and this is Deanna Hovland. Deanna is our colleague in Illinois. She's here for a couple of weeks helping us out."

"Pleased to meet you ladies. Shall we?" Bob said as he held the restaurant door for the girls.

"Ladies," Bob said as they were sitting down, "I'd like to buy your lunch today. I'm honored to help you research my great-granddad. I suppose that should be a couple of greats, huh? Well, let's have lunch before we get too deep in thought." Just as the county clerk had said, the Welton family was still farming in the area.

During lunch Bob brought out a letter from a relative in Nebraska. Bob's cousin stated in the letter that Ben Alt had died in 1923 and was buried in Lincoln, Nebraska. There was also a record of pensions being received by Alt. How could the files on the website not have this information? Bob thought that he had seen a Civil War framed discharge at his grandmother's house when he was young. He had no idea what happened to it. Samantha and Deanna were impressed with the information Bob had with him.

The pension statements Bob had were issued out of the Lincoln pension agent's office and were in the amount of $24.00 per quarter. Deanna knew that that amount was consistent with pensions paid after 1881.

Everything looked legitimate. Samantha said, "Everything looks great. The pension office may not have forwarded all the records to Washington. I still don't understand why Alt's discharge wasn't recorded. If that's the real case, there might be hundreds or thousands of discharge records missing. We may never know."

After lunch and their exchange of information, Samantha and Deanna thanked Bob for his time and assistance in their research and for buying lunch. Bob was delighted to help out. "Heck," Bob said with a chuckle, "I don't get to dine with two lovely young ladies very often. Thank you for taking such an interest in my kin. I've enjoyed this very much."

On the way back to Sussex, Samantha wanted to show Deanna the village of Farmer's Retreat. It wasn't out of the way and the girls had time to spare. "This is a neat place, Deanna. When Morgan's Raiders invaded this part of Indiana, the farmers fled their farms and hid over the hills. Many of the farmers built temporary shelters here and because some of the families felt safer here they stayed until the end of the war. As you can see, some of them never went back to their farms." Deanna was beginning to like the flavor of this part of the country. It had a deep history.

Gabe was in his office when Samantha and Deanna returned. "Well," he said as he greeted them, "did you met with Mr. Welton?"

Samantha handed Gabe her notepad and said, "Yes we did, and he had a handful of information for us. As you can see, he had pension records, dates, and a death record from Nebraska. Mr. Welton also says he remembers seeing a discharge at his grandmother's house years ago. I'd say that's good enough to claim we found Ben Alt. Wouldn't you say so?" Gabe quickly scanned Samantha's notes.

Looking up at Deanna and Samantha, he nodded in agreement. "Yes, I would say so; that's another one down. Now, why don't you two head back to your place, Samantha, and I'll finish up here? I'll pick you up at 5:30 and we'll go out to Fuller's for dinner. We'll celebrate. Are you up for that?"

Samantha's reply was instant; "You'll get no argument from me. We're outta of here. See ya' at 5:30."

Dinner was very relaxing. Deanna really enjoyed the atmosphere and rustic charm of Fuller's. Gabe asked Samantha, "Where are the two of you headed for the rest of the week?" Samantha had a small steno pad in front of her at the table.

"Tomorrow we are planning to see Reverend David Fuller at the Methodist Church in Morrefield at 9:30. Dr. Carls had established that Corporal Hayes' family had lived there for some time before the war. The church may have records for us to look at. I called Reverend Fuller right before we left for Indy and he said he would dig out the records and have them for us tomorrow. If we get out of there fairly early, by noon maybe, I thought we'd take a run to Vevay and meet with Gene Fife. Gene said to call first and make sure he'll be there. That should take up all of tomorrow.

"I thought I would contact Daviess County and see if they came up with any conclusive evidence on Private Blocker. We know he has family in Montgomery. Dr. Carls has notes saying that the county records showed him dying in 1893. I can check this one out over the phone. Finally, I think on Thursday we can go over to Aberdeen and search the city hall records for Private Bean. We should find what we need to close his file. I talked to the local historian and he thinks he saw something conclusive in their records years ago. And that should just about bring us to the weekend."

Gabe glanced up from his dessert, looked at Deanna and said, "Well, sounds like you're going to see a lot of our scenery the next couple of days. Good, you have a plan. I have a couple of things I want to accomplish this week, too. I thought I'd tackle Sergeant Bendalone and Corporal Carr. I'll have the whole office to myself while you're gone. I can't wait to get into that G.A.R. website. A little old-fashioned research sounds like fun. Okay then, Samantha, you get to buy the next round. We have a couple of hours yet, let's make the most of it before you two have to hit the sack. You have a full day ahead of you."

Gabe danced the night away with both of his "dates." Deanna tried to let the two of them have some time together alone. Not being a wallflower, Deanna had no trouble asking single men to dance. It was a memorable evening.

Samantha turned off Route 129 onto the gravel road that led to Moorefield. This was a very old town. Most of the buildings had been abandoned years ago. The current population was only about 500 at best. "Looks creepy, Samantha,"

Deanna observed. The Methodist church was a wood-framed structure, painted white and in need of a fresh coat. The weather was bone chilling chilly as the girls exited the car. The cold wind seemed to go right through their coats.

The temperature inside the church was nearly equal to that outside. The lights were off and the silence was deafening. "Hello!" cried Samantha. "Reverend Fuller, are you here?"

The door behind the altar was ajar. The only light in the church beamed through the small crack. A medium-sized man with black hair and a slight build came out and greeted the girls. "Hi, I'm David Fuller. Sorry about the heat in here. I didn't get in early enough to turn up the furnace. It'll kick on in a minute. Come on into the office. I found some really old record for you in our storage facility over in Versailles. As you can see, we don't keep anything of real value here. No room to store anything. I cover three congregations, so you can imagine me hauling things from church to church. Oh, I'm sorry, would either of you like some coffee. I have a fresh pot in the kitchen."

"Yes, I would," answered Samantha.

Deanna, who rarely drinks coffee, followed Samantha's lead and said, "Yes, me too." The hot coffee cups helped to warm their hands.

In the office, Reverend Fuller delicately opened the old bound records book. The first entry was November 14, 1856. "Wow," said Deanna. "This congregation goes pretty far back."

"Yes," said Reverend Fuller. "This is the oldest Methodist congregation in southern Indiana. At one time it was the largest as well. Today, we only see an average of twenty to twenty-five worshippers on Sunday. As you have seen, the town is smaller now. Lots of empty homes."

Reverend Fuller turned to the marker he had put on page six. "Here, I found the name of the family you mentioned to me, Samantha. David Wayne Hayes, baptized March 8,

1857, aged 13 years 3 months. That means he was born in say January 1844 or so, right?"

"I think that's the same guy we're looking for. If he enlisted in 1862 that would make him eighteen years old. Sounds right. What else can we find?" Reverend Fuller turned to page seventy-one. Dust from the book plumed into the air as he turned the pages. "I found another entry too. It's hard to read this old writing. The style of writing is one thing, but the fading of the ink makes it that much harder. I think this says that Hayes was killed in Virginia in 1864. Here, you look at it and see what you think those words are. They're barely visible."

Samantha and Deanna leaned over the book. Deanna sneezed from the dust. "Excuse me," she offered. Both girls strained their eyes. Samantha tended to agree with Reverend Fuller's interpretation.

Deanna agreed, but she thought there was more, as the text seemed to continue on the next page. On page seventy-two were the names of family funerals for the month of June 1864. Deanna read on. She asked if there had been an outbreak of flu or something that anyone knew about. There were five funerals for "Infant" children. Then, as if by providence, she saw it. In plain letters, faded, but legible, *Service for David Hayes, June 14, 1864, no body, buried in Willis, Virginia, died of consumption.* The words were barely visible. Samantha and Deanna sat motionless. The text continued, . . . *only father John attended...mother too distraught.*

The small hamlet of Moorefield had sent two of its youths to war. Neither of them came home. Moorefield suffered the same fate as countless other small towns of that time. Now, the record of David Hayes could be closed. Samantha had found the evidence she needed. It was so close to where the hunt began, but buried in an old forgotten book, covered with age-old dust.

Samantha and Deanna thanked Reverend Fuller for his time and for the job he was doing with this historic congregation. Reverend Fuller said he would use the information on David Hayes in his sermon. It would be a real inspiration to his worshippers to know of his service and sacrifice.

Deanna was writing notes as Samantha drove. Vevay was only about twenty miles away. They stopped at Marilyn's Café as they drove back through Sussex to use the phone to call Gene Fife and get a beverage to drink in the car. Marilyn offered some freshly baked cookies to Deanna while Samantha was on the phone. "Here, hun, you girls need something to warm you up on a day like today. Tuesday's are always our slowest days. I'd hate to have these cookies sittin' here gettin' stale, and I don't need to be here eatin' them all."

Deanna thanked Marilyn as she took the small white bag of cookies. Samantha returned from the phone and said, "Gene will meet us at the records center in an hour. We're invited to his house for lunch. We'll get to meet Dorothy. Dr. Carls says her cooking is wonderful."

Marilyn caught Samantha's comments, "Now listen you two, if you can get me a recipe for some good stuff it'd be appreciated. Here me now?" The girls just laughed as they headed out the door.

Gene was sitting at his desk when Samantha and Deanna arrived. "Hello, come on in."

Samantha introduced herself and Deanna. Aside from working with Gene nearly two years ago, Samantha had talked to Gene on the phone several times. Samantha asked to see the old brown box again. Gene had moved it, along with some papers I had looked at, to a steel cabinet. Deanna sat at a gray steel table.

Gene placed the box on the table and told the girls not to get too involved since Dorothy had lunch planned for 12:30. Samantha and Deanna just smiled. Deanna began emptying the contents of the box, just as I had done last winter.

She immediately found the tri-fold pension document. Samantha reached for the document saying, "Let me see that. How did I miss that two years ago?"

Gene glanced at his watch. "Okay ladies, lunch is served. I'm driving, so let's load up. Dorothy won't hold lunch on ya' now. You're in for a treat. I think she even made her famous baked apples. I don't even get those. When we get back here I got something for you gals. I talked to a friend of mine at a meeting two weeks ago. He has some info for ya'. I'll give him a call. He's expecting to talk to one of you today."

Gene and Dorothy's house was just as I had described it to Deanna. Dorothy had the dining-room table set with her best china. She even had her finest crystal glassware out.

Gene commented, "My gosh, Dot, you set up for the Pope himself. We haven't had the special settings out since Jake's wedding party in '85."

Dorothy gave a look that only a wife of fifty years can. "Gene," she scolded, "seat our guests and yourself now. Lunch is ready for the eatin'."

Samantha just loved the house with the old overstuffed chairs and sofa. She commented to Dorothy, "I love all the doilies you have."

As she served her homemade asparagus soup, Dorothy answered, "I made most of those myself when I was a little girl. I went to a one-room school and Miss Ericsson was my teacher. She was Norwegian and she taught all the girls and a couple of the boys how to crochet. I remember we crocheted a lot during the winter months to keep our hands warm. She told us the faster we crocheted, the more blood we got to our fingers. I don't remember getting warmer, but I know I made a lot of doilies."

Deanna talked about Sycamore and her work at the university. Dorothy and Gene were genuinely interested.

Dorothy asked Deanna, "When is that nice Mr. Carls coming back down this way? He said he was coming this fall."

Deanna responded, "Oh, I don't know, maybe that's why I'm here instead. I know he talked about coming back here though."

"Well," said Dorothy, "I like that man. He seems very honest and a hard worker, too."

Deanna concluded, "Yes, he gets a lot done. He's really enjoying this project we're involved with now. I think he realizes how long this may take. I know he, all of us, appreciate all that Gene has been able to help us with. And of course, your cooking, Dorothy, is unforgettable. I think he may come back even after we're done, just for one of your meals." Dorothy dropped her chin and blushed.

Deanna insisted on helping clean up and doing the dishes with Dorothy.

Gene took Samantha on a house tour as such and showed her the family photos in the hallway. "Now here's Jake, our number two guy. He's thirty-three, an engineer over in Cincinnati. He's the one that got married in '85; lovely little wife, Barbara. Bob here is thirty-nine. Wife's name is Diane, lives in Omaha with our twin granddaughters. This here is John, the baby. He's twenty-seven. We always teased him about being our accident son. He's a stockbroker in New York; busy guy, rarely see him. Still single if either of you gals are interested."

As soon as they returned to the records center, Gene placed a call to Eugene Roberts, a county clerk friend in Crawfordsville, Montgomery County. His name was Eugene Roberts. Gene explained as he was dialing, "Eugene here found a name on your list while he was researching a documentary on one-room school houses for the State Board of Education. He's got a great story for ya'. I'll let him tell ya' when he picks up here." The phone rang about ten times. Finally, Gene says, "Hello, this Eugene? This is Gene Fife in Vevay. I got those young ladies here I told you about. Why don't you tell them about that teacher fella in Darlington?"

Gene handed the phone to Deanna. "Hello, Mr. Roberts, this is Deanna Hovland from Moss University. What do you think you found for us in, where was it, Darlington?"

"Hi, Deanna. I'm doing some research for a documentary on one-room schoolhouses for the state. I ran across a name that Gene there gave me. A man by the name of William Wollman was one of our teachers here in Montgomery County. We know he was a veteran. He taught in Darlington for about ten years. Our records show he never married. He would have been born about 1843 or so. The really interesting thing I told Gene is that he is buried on the school grounds."

Deanna said, "Ewe!"

Eugene continued, "If he's your guy, I can fax this paper to you right now. There is some other information here that may be of help to you."

Deanna said, "Sure, go ahead and fax it. And thank you very much."

"No problem, Deanna. I'll hang up here. It's all on one line ya' know. Good luck with the rest of your search. Say good-bye to Gene for me. Tell him I'll be in touch."

It took about ten minutes for the fax to arrive. Deanna picked up the two sheets of paper and began to read. "It says that he was in the Veteran Corps from 1865 to December 1871. That means he was part of the occupational troops during reconstruction in the South.

Samantha listened and then remembered something. "Now I get it. He wouldn't show up as being mustered out of service with the other regular regiments. That's why he isn't on one of our lists. He reenlisted. When he transferred to the 27th Indiana in '64, we assumed he was discharged from that unit as well. He must have enlisted in the Veteran Corps after the

27th was dissolved. It would probably have been handled as another transfer in order to pay him the active duty rate. It all makes sense to me now."

Deanna looked at Gene and shrugged her shoulders saying, "If you say so. Sounds good to me. Can you sell Mr. Carls on it?"

"Sure," Samantha replied. "I've seen this before when Gabe did his dissertation. I never thought about the missing soldiers reenlisting as veterans. Their records are completely different from the regular wartime troops. Even the official records of the war classify the Veteran Corps differently. Unless you know exactly what you're looking for, you'll never find it in the official records. I think Mr. Roberts found this guy for us. Let's call Dr. Carls and tell him."

I was very pleased to here about Private Wollman and Corporal Hayes. I could hardly believe that they had found two soldiers in one day. To tell the truth, I was shocked. The evidence was unmistakable. The files on these two soldiers could be closed. Our list was shrinking.

After calling me, Gene handed Samantha the transfer document from the waxed box. "I know," said Samantha. "How on earth did I not see this? I thought I went through everything in here. It certainly would have saved us a lot of time and trouble if I'd had these names. I think we can still track down a few more of these guys by looking at muster records from their transfer units. I see at least four names we haven't located yet."

Gene went to lock the door at 4:30. Deanna and Samantha said their good-byes and took with them the satisfaction of finding another soldier. They particularly enjoyed lunch with Dorothy and their grandfatherly talk with Gene. "Give our best to Dorothy and tell her thanks again," Deanna said.

Gene turned from the door and in leaving told the girls, "Drive carefully now. It gets dark early and those winding roads can be treacherous."

Gabe was just turning off the office lights when Samantha came down the stairs. "And how was your day?" Samantha asked.

Gabe replied, "It was very productive. How was yours? Find anything?

Samantha waited for Deanna before responding, "Yes we did, two soldiers!"

Gabe beamed and replied, "Me too. I just love that G.A.R. site. Bingo, you can cross off Carr and Davidson. They both made careers in the service and stayed active until the 1880s. We were looking for discharges twenty years too early."

Samantha and Deanna were very impressed. Four finds in one day. Incredible!

Deanna slept in on Wednesday. Samantha had to cover a class for an instructor who would be out of town for the day. Later she was going to call a local historian in Montgomery about Private Bean. He was supposed to have some information on him for her today. Deanna lay on the sofa under an afghan. It was warm and cuddly there. Looking out the window from the sofa, Deanna could see that it had started to snow. The temperature was such that none of the snow was sticking. Deanna turned on the T.V. and relaxed.

Samantha called at noon. Deanna had fallen back asleep and the ringing of the phone startled her. "Hello," she said as if programmed, "Samantha's residence."

"Deanna," Samantha replied, "This is Sam. I'll pick you up for lunch in twenty minutes. Can you be ready?"

"I guess so," answered Deanna, somewhat groggy.

"Good," answered Samantha, "I have to meet Dr. Brackett at Julie's Restaurant at 1:00. It's just south of town. I want you to meet him. I'll honk out front; be ready."

Deanna was ready and Samantha was on time. Deanna literally jumped into the car. Samantha looked at Deanna and then out the rear window of her car as she pulled away from the curb. "You gotta meet this guy," she began. "His name is Jim Brackett. He's visiting from Indiana State. I told him about you. He's a great guy."

Deanna rolled her eyes and replied, "Samantha, look at me. I'm not ready to meet anybody for the first time. Thanks."

"Nonsense," said Samantha, "you look great. It's just for lunch anyway. Say hi, see what happens."

Julie's Restaurant was an old café along the road, seating twenty-five or thirty customers at most. Julie herself did the cooking. The tables were chrome dinette sets. "I hear the food's good," Samantha said as they pulled into the parking lot. Deanna made no response. She still felt uncomfortable about the whole situation.

Inside they met Dr. Brackett at a table near the back corner. "Hi, Samantha," he greeted them.

"Hi, Jim. This is Deanna."

"Nice to meet you, Jim." Deanna was noticeably uncomfortable.

As they sat down, Jim volunteered an explanation for wanting to meet Deanna. "I hear you're from Moss University." Deanna nodded. "Well," Jim continued, "I sent my resume to Dr. Joanne Darling. I understand you know her, right?"

Again, Deanna nodded in agreement. Jim asked, "What can you tell me about her?"

Deanna was hesitant to say anything about a colleague. "I work with Dr. Darling on occasion," replied Deanna. "She brings a great deal of work to our research department. She really knows her field; is a very nice person. What do you want me to say?"

"No, no," replied Jim, "I only want to get some sort of a feel for her. I applied for a staff position at Moss and I have an interview with Dr. Darling next Thursday. I thought maybe you could give me some idea of what to expect."

Deanna continued, "She's very fair and I'd say just be yourself and be honest. She expects hard work from her people. I do a lot of work with David Hinman, her grad assistant. She keeps him busy all the time."

"Fair enough," said Dr. Brackett. "That's all I can ask. I always hate these interview things; they drive me nuts. Now, I'm interested in hearing more about the research you two are doing. Can you tell me about it?"

"Sure," offered Deanna. "It all started with an article Dr. Warren had in a magazine about missing Civil War soldiers. We have an experimental Internet development site at Moss. Dr. Carls, my boss, contacted Samantha and Dr. Warren about working together using our system to help find the missing soldiers. That was about a year ago. Now we've located about half of them, I think. It's been fun and a real learning experience. We're finding out what the Internet system can do. It's going to be a great thing in the future. I think schools will go crazy with it."

"I've heard of the system, Deanna, but when do you think the general public will get to use it?" asked Jim. "Are you seeing, what do you call them, sites, on the system yet?"

Samantha answered, "Yes, more than I thought there would be. The newest one is huge. It's the G.A.R. site. It has millions of entries on Civil War veterans, everything from service records, to discharges, to pension records. We've been spending a lot of time thumbing through those sites. It's all very time-consuming. It will take us another year to find the remaining soldiers."

Jim was impressed. "Do you have designated time to work on the project?" he asked.

"No." Samantha offered, "We pretty much do it in our free time. Dr. Carls is the one who has leave time just for the project. You know he has an NSC grant for the project?"

"Ladies, I wish you the best," Jim said as he stood up from the table. "I better be heading back. Next week will be here soon enough. I have to get my head together for Dr. Darling. Now you, Deanna, may be seeing more of me if all goes well. My research area is in medicine. I'll probably have some work for you and Dr. Carls to do. I hope it turns out that way; I'd like to work with you. Thanks for meeting with me and for sharing info on Dr. Darling. Be careful driving back. The snow looks like it's starting to stick."

With that said, Samantha and Deanna started their drive back to Sussex. The snow was beginning to stick. However, it was no deeper than an inch.

Gabe was getting off the phone when Deanna and Samantha returned to the office. "How did your lunch go with Jim Brackett?" he asked. "He seems like a fairly nice guy. I hear you might have him on staff at Moss, Deanna."

Deanna rolled her eyes at Gabe and simply replied, "We'll see."

Gabe turned to Samantha saying, "I just placed an ad in the *Louisville Courier-Journal*. I listed the names of the remaining soldiers and asked if anyone was related to them or knew anything about them. Maybe we can get a response instead of covering all those counties on foot. I listed the hotel we're staying at in case someone locally wants to leave a message for us."

Samantha thought that was a good idea. Her only comment to Gabe was, "That's one way of doing it."

Deanna helped herself to the project files and a Diet Coke. She spread the files out on the table and made herself as comfortable as possible. Gabe was on his computer doing class work. Samantha sat at her desk and rummaged for a phone number to the Daviess county clerk's office. She had written the number on an index card and thought she put it in the top drawer of her desk. Unfortunately, that drawer was a catchall. It seemed everything went there for safekeeping.

"Where can that number be?" Samantha kept digging. Finally, she found it in the rear of the drawer. As she dialed the phone, she was asking herself, *what's his name*? She had failed to write down the clerk's name. When she spoke to him last, she had given him the name of James Blocker, Sergeant, Co. C, 14th Indiana Infantry and that he had died in 1893. The clerk had remembered either seeing or hearing that name before. Today, Samantha wanted to know if he had found any additional information for her.

A man picked up the phone and said, "Daviess county clerk's office, may I help you?"

Samantha sighed and said, "Ah yes, this is Samantha Martinson from Oglethorpe Christian College, and I..."

The man interrupted her, "Yes, Miss Martinson, this is Charles Smith. I spoke to you a few weeks ago about a Civil War soldier. I may have something for you. Just a minute, please." Samantha was relieved that he had introduced himself.

"Miss Martinson," Charles said as he picked the phone back up. "We have a note here in our files that states a replacement marker was issued for Private James Blocker in November of 1950. The note is from the U.S. Bureau of Monuments. Private Blocker is buried in Arlington in Section 244, Block 11, Row 9, Marker 16. That's all I have here. I don't see anything like discharge or pension records. I hope that can help you in your search."

Samantha was jotting down the information as fast as Mr. Smith was talking. "Yes, Mr. Smith, thank you, that will help me a great deal. Thank you again for your time; it's really appreciated."

Charles replied before hanging up, "Anything else you need Miss Martinson, just call. Nice talking to you again."

"Can you believe it," Samantha blurted out, "Blocker is buried in Arlington National Cemetery and we can't find a discharge on the guy. How did that happen?"

Gabe and Deanna stopped what they were doing. Gabe took off his glasses and began biting on the earpiece. "Strange, isn't it?" Gabe offered. "I looked yesterday for Blocker in the G.A.R. files while you were at Gene's. I ran his name in all states. Nothing. No membership anywhere. I was going to suggest that he must have been left on the field dead. That still may be the case. But how would he end up in Washington? Doesn't make sense to me. What else do you have, Sam?"

"Well, I have a location and a date of death. They also have a note from the Bureau of Monuments in 1950 for a new headstone. I never knew they replaced Civil War headstones unless the soldiers were overlooked when the stones were issued the first time. Can we research when stones were issued?"

Deanna jumped into the conversation, "Yes, we can. Let's check for a website for the bureau first. If there is no website, I know I have a directory back home. I think the government issued headstones for Union veterans up through the 1930s. Those were the small round-topped markers with the badge in the middle. You've seen them. They all look alike. Let's punch up a website name and see if there is anything."

Gabe typed in bureauofmonuments.org. Nothing. He tried monuments.com. Nothing again. Again he tried, civilwarburialmarkers.com. Nothing. "Nothing here," he concluded.

Deanna replied, "I'll look it up when I get home. Ya' know what, I'll have Mr. Carls bring that book to Terre Haute next week."

"Gabe," Samantha asked, "why don't you look and see if there's a site for Arlington National Cemetery? There has to be a directory somewhere."

Gabe swiveled in his chair and typed arlingtonnationalcem etery.org. The screen on his computer darkened and then came back up. The words across the top of the screen read, ARLINGTON NATIONAL CEMETERY. "We're in," Gabe said as he turned toward Samantha. "I have several options. Let's see. DIRECTORY." Gabe typed in BLOCKER, JAMES. The computer flashed, WHAT ACTION. Gabe typed, CIVIL WAR. The screen turned black as the computer clicked away. Then the screen lit up with green text. WHAT STATE. Gabe entered, INDIANA. Again the screen darkened and the clicking began.

When the text reappeared, there was a list with hundreds of names. Next to each name was the date of internment, section number, block number, and row number within the cemetery. The names were listed in order by date of internment.

Gabe printed the list. It took seven pages of green-bar paper to complete the list. Deanna helped Samantha lay out the sheets. The girls began looking for 1893 dates. Samantha ran her finger down the page. "Wow," she said, "lot of funerals in July. Okay, here's November. Blocker, Blocker, Blocker. No Blocker. Now that's weird. We know he's there but no Blocker is listed. What do you make of that?"

Gabe joined them looking at the list. "Alright, let's start at the top and go down the entire list. Maybe your county clerk friend has the wrong month written down."

All three of them scoured the list. No James Blocker from Indiana. "Why isn't he here?" said Deanna. "Something's not right."

Samantha went to Gabe's desk and dialed the number for Daviess County. "Mr. Charles Smith, please." she asked the operator.

"Charles Smith, may I help you?"

"Mr. Smith, this is Samantha Martinson again. About the information on James Blocker: Might you have been wrong on the month of his burial? You told me November, right?"

"No, that's incorrect. I only know that there was a new headstone issued to him in November of 1950. The note I have does not say when he was buried. You had told me that he died in 1893. At least that's what I wrote down after our first conversation. Did you contact Arlington for confirmation?"

"No, we looked on the new Internet website for Arlington and they don't have him listed at all. Where do you think the note you have came from in the first place?"

"I don't know. I looked in our Civil War categories and files, and there it was. It isn't signed or anything. I think the note must be twenty-five or thirty years old."

"Wow, that's interesting. Do you know who would have been in charge of records at that time?"

"Sure, old Bob Greene. He died about six years ago. I took over shortly after."

"Okay, Mr. Smith. I'll try to contact Arlington directly and see what they have in their records. Thank you again for all your help. Bye now."

"Well, that was fun. Charlie Smith doesn't have anything but the date a new headstone was erected. And as far as that goes, who would have requested a new stone in the first place?"

Gabe sat back in his chair and took off his glasses. He closed his eyes and appeared in deep thought. "Now," he finally said, "let's think this through. We know that his death certificate says he died in a private hospital in 1893. If I remember right, his family was from Washington, Indiana. Tell you what, check out the drive to Washington and if you two can, go there tomorrow and see if there are any local records at city hall or maybe a church."

Samantha immediately asked, "Aren't we going to Louisville this weekend?"

"Yes we are," Gabe assured her, "but that's Friday afternoon. You can make a day of it tomorrow. You'll be back by dinnertime."

"Alright, we'll check it out. I didn't have anything planned for tomorrow anyway. We'll leave right after breakfast. It isn't that long of a drive."

Deanna just sat there. She was agreeable.

"Deanna," Samantha said, "Washington is a little over an hour's drive from here. Why don't we go do our shopping now so we can get an early start tomorrow?"

Samantha and Deanna left Gabe at the office. They were headed for a sale at Maryann's clothing store. Deanna had seen a couple of cute tops she wanted to pick up before her trip to Terre Haute.

Gabe called directory assistance and asked for the main number at Arlington National Cemetery. The actual address was listed as Arlington, Virginia. The phone rang several times before someone answered. "Front Gate, Sergeant Moore speaking."

"Yes, Sergeant, can you direct me to someone who may have information on burial records?"

"Yes, sir, that would be Staff Sergeant Wilkin. Please hold."

"Staff Sergeant Wilkin, may I help you?"

"Staff Sergeant Wilkin, my name is Gabe Warren, and I am doing research for the National Science Commission. I am trying to locate a Civil War veteran buried there in Arlington. Can you help me verify his grave site?"

"Should be no problem sir, What is the name?"

"James Blocker, 14th Indiana Volunteer Infantry. I believe the burial would have been in 1893."

"Thank you, this should just take a moment."

The phone was silent for a couple of minutes.

"Sir, you said you were doing research for the National Science Commission, is that right?"

"Yes, that's right. I have a location if that helps."

"And what would that be, sir?"

"Section 244, Block 11, Row 9, Marker 16."

"Sir, that section of the cemetery is not accessible according to my computer. I don't know why that would be."

"How can a section of the cemetery be inaccessible?"

"I don't know, sir. I've never encountered this before. I'll look into it for you though. May I have your number and I'll call you back?"

Gabe gave the sergeant his number and then he went about his work, not expecting a call back for some time.

Samantha and Deanna were at the door waiting for Marilyn to open the café. It was 6:45. The sun wouldn't be up for nearly an hour. Samantha really wanted to get on the road early. Marilyn greeted the early birds, "You ladies must have a big day ahead of you to be up this early?"

"We're driving over to Washington in Daviess County. I want to get back before dark," Samantha answered.

Deanna wasn't really awake. She ordered her usual, a large orange juice and wheat toast. Samantha had a full breakfast. They were on the road by 8:00.

Gabe got to Draper Hall shortly before 8:00. He was usually the first person in the building, but not today. There was a note taped to the glass on the office door. It read, Dr. Warren, please call Krista Butler at NSC Headquarters, Ext. 618. The message was taken at 4:55 p.m., just before the switchboard closed for the day on Wednesday.

Gabe waited until 8:30 and called me at my office. He told me about contacting Arlington National Cemetery and his conversation with the sergeant. He was very concerned about this message from Krista Butler. I told him to go ahead and return her call and see what she had to say. I explained to him that she might want to know about how our research was going using the Internet. I told him not to worry and just tell her we were following up on the information from the Daviess county clerk's office.

Gabe dialed the number and Krista's extension. She answered immediately. "Krista Butler."

"Miss Butler, this is Gabe Warren at Oglethorpe Christian College. I missed your call yesterday afternoon."

"Yes, Dr. Warren. I received a call from security at Arlington Cemetery yesterday afternoon."

Gabe interrupted, "From security?"

"Yes, Dr. Warren, from security. It seems you made an inquiry into a sensitive area of the cemetery."

"How sensitive can a grave location be?"

"Well, sir, that depends. What are you looking for?"

"Miss Butler, you know what Dr. Carls and his team are looking for, just some lost Civil War soldiers. How is that a security issue?"

"Dr. Warren, you mentioned to the sergeant that you were doing research for the NSC. That is not true. You're doing the research for yourselves. Dr. Carls knows the NSC is monitoring the Internet use. Our interest is only how the Internet is being used, not what you're researching."

"Fine, Miss Butler. That's all well and good. All I know is I asked the sergeant if he could confirm a grave location and the next thing I know, you're calling me about security. What's with that?"

"Dr. Warren, don't worry about it. You ran into an area that the government feels is not in the realm of your research. The records at Arlington are nothing to be concerned about. You have your soldier's name and burial information. Cross him off your list and move on."

"What," Gabe blurted in a raised voice, "what do you mean the *government* feels it's out of our realm? Is there more to this than you're telling us?"

"No, Dr. Warren, I'm just telling you in another way that the information you have on James Blocker is correct. There is no need for you to continue looking here for more. I'll be talking to Dr. Carls in a few days. I'll explain more to him at that time. I have to go now. Good luck with the rest of your research. I hope this hasn't changed your view of the NSC. We're here to help you in any way we can. Nice talking to you, Dr. Warren. Have a good day."

Gabe hung up the phone and took a deep breath. Gabe called me immediately and told me about Krista's comments. I was somewhat surprised. If the NSC was going to help us with our research, they had a funny way to show it. My suspicions of Miss Butler seemed to be founded. I continued doing my own searches at Moss and waited the next couple of days for Krista's call.

Meanwhile, Samantha and Deanna were nearing Washington. It had snowed about an inch during the night in Daviess County but the roads were clear by the time they got there.

It was only 9:10 when they arrived in downtown Washington. The city hall offices wouldn't open until 9:30. Samantha parked the car and they went into the small café across the street. After sitting in a corner booth, the girls ordered hot chocolates and waited for the city hall to open.

Samantha asked Deanna, "Just what are we going to ask for here? Do you really think Blocker has family around here anymore? Let's get the phone book and look there."

Deanna got up from the table and headed for the pay phone across the room. She stood there for perhaps three or four minutes before she waved for Samantha to join her.

"Look, there's a Robert J. Blocker on North Cross Street. Why don't we call him first? It isn't too early, is it?"

Deanna dialed the number. Robert Blocker answered right away.

"Mr. Blocker?" Deanna asked. "My name is Deanna Hovland. I'm doing research on Civil War soldiers. Do you mind if I ask you a question or two about your family?"

"No, ma'am, I don't mind. I don't know if I had any family that fought in that war though."

"Well, sir, I have the name of a James Blocker from here in Indiana. He was with the 14th Indiana Infantry. I know he died around 1893."

"Whoa, ma'am, you're asking me if I know anything about this James Blocker fella?"

"Yes, sir."

"Well, I don't know about that. I've never heard about it from any family before. I suppose I can ask my grandmother though. She's ninety-two years old. I guess if anyone in the family knows anything about that it would be her."

"I would greatly appreciate it if you can do that, sir. I'm in Washington right now and I'll be at city hall today. I can give you my office number where you can reach me, is that okay?"

"Sure, but I'm only about four blocks from you now. I can call my brother's house, that's where Grandma lives now. I may have an answer for you in a while. I don't think she gets up until 9:30 or so. I may even run up to city hall in a bit if you'll be there."

"Thank you, Mr. Blocker. I'd enjoy meeting you. I'd also like to tell you about our research a bit more too."

"That'd be great. I'm really interested in history. I'm surprised no one ever mentioned anything about a relative in the Civil War before. Well, I'll see what I can find out for you. I'll either see you or talk at you real soon. Take care now."

Deanna and Samantha finished their drinks and walked to city hall.

Washington City Hall is a rather small building considering the size of Washington. The elderly lady at the front desk greeted Samantha and Deanna. "Good morning, ladies.

May I help you?"

"Yes," Samantha replied. "We're from Oglethorpe Christian College in Sussex. We're interested in any information you may have on Civil War veterans from here in Washington."

"Well, let's see. I believe you'll have to talk to Mr. Barker in records. He's here; I just passed him in the rear hall coming in this morning. I'll walk you back to his area."

The walk back to the records area was relatively short. The walls were painted a dark green. The lighting was inadequate.
We came to the end of the hall and turned into a small room. There, standing behind a desk and watering a healthy African violet plant was who must have been Mr. Barker.

"Good morning, Mr. Barker. We have guests from Sussex today. These young ladies are looking for information on Civil War soldiers from Washington. I'll let them ask the questions. Oh, would either of you care for a cup of coffee?"

Deanna was quick to reply. "No, ma'am, we just had breakfast and coffee across the street, but thank you for asking."

"Hi, Mr. Barker, I'm Samantha Martinson and this is Deanna Hovland. Do you know of any Civil War records you may have here related to the 14th Indiana Infantry? We're looking for any information on a James Blocker?"

"Blocker, I know that name. They're still here in town."

"Yes, we talked to Robert Blocker. He lives on North Cross."

"Yes, that's the family. I know his mother, Lillian. She's up there in age now. I'll take a look for you. Miss Lillian may know some family history for you too."

Mr. Barker walked across the little room. It couldn't have been more than twelve feet square. He had two old, brown file cabinets in one corner. He pulled out the third drawer from the top and he fumbled through several files. "Ah, here it is. Article in the *Daily Chronicle* from November 1950. The Blocker family received notification that Private James Blocker was laid to rest in Arlington National Cemetery on the 17th. It says here that the body was discovered down south. It doesn't say where. Here, you ladies take a look."

Samantha reached for the old newspaper article. "Look Deanna, it says a *burial*, not just a headstone replacement."

Deanna read the article and asked, "Samantha, what does this mean?"

"I'm not sure."

"Mr. Barker, may I make a copy of this article for our project?"

"Why sure, missy; it's just an old article. You look a little surprised. Anything wrong?"

Deanna turned to Mr. Barker. "No, nothing wrong."

Samantha inquired about any additional information.

"Well, I have a list of veterans. I'll make you a copy of that as well."

Samantha told Mr. Barker that they were going to possibly talk to Lillian Blocker later in the day. For now, they settled for a copy of the article and a list of local vets.

Mr. Barker walked the girls out of the building and pointed to a city park two blocks down the main street. "Now down at the park there's a statue with a plaque you may be interested in reading. I can't remember exactly what it says, but you'll enjoy it. When you're done there, be sure to stop in at the Blue Star Hardware Store and ask for Andy. He's our local Civil War buff. He can answer most questions you might have."

It was so chilly; Samantha drove the two blocks to the park. The statue was of a single soldier knelling down and loading his gun. It was bronze, and green from aging. The contrasting green and brown colors made for an interesting figure. The facial features had great eminence and were foreboding. The figure's eyes were hollow and seemed to follow no matter where you moved.

The plaque at the base of the statue was about twenty inches in length and ten inches high. The letters had turned dark green with tarnish many years ago and made it difficult to read.

Deanna knelt down and brushed away the snow. Then she rubbed away the dirt from the letters. The plaque read:

> *Dedicated to our fallen Fathers, Sons and Brothers*
> *who gave their last full measure*
> *of devotion to preserve our union.*

Present and Accounted For

*The citizens of Daviess County and the City of Washington
pay tribute in your honor and to your
memory.*

Here dedicated

May 27, 1911

*Erected by the Women's Relief Corps
and G.A.R. Garber Post #72*

Samantha read the words out loud and then said, "Nice statue; nothing here for us though."

Deanna stood up and brushed the snow from her slacks. As they turned around to head for the car, Deanna saw a large boulder in the corner at the opposite end of the park. It appeared to have a plaque mounted on it.

Samantha went to the car to warm it up while Deanna walked across the park to look at the stone. Most of the small green plaque was hidden behind a bush that stood in front of the stone. Deanna parted the branches.

The writing on the bronze tablet was in fine script and the spaces of the letters were caked with years of mud. Deanna tried to read as much as she could. It was a difficult task. In the meantime, Samantha pulled the car around the corner and parked near Deanna and the stone.

Samantha rolled down her window and asked, "What does it say?"

"I can't read it all, but it has five names on it. They're caked in mud. Come look at this."

Samantha got out of the car but left it running. When she got close to the stone, she bent over to read the inscription. "I'll get something out of my car and see if we can scrape the mud off." She grabbed her snow scraper with stiff bristles on one end.

When Samantha returned, she and Deanna worked on the mud. It was cold and windy now. Their hands were freezing. Then Deanna made out one of the names. It said *Abraham Wheeler*. Another name appeared from the mud, *Jacob Martin*. As they rubbed away more mud, more names appeared: *John Bethell*, *Marcus Grime*, and to their utter surprise, *James Blocker*. The two girls looked at each other in shock.

Deanna turned to Samantha and in a solemn tone said, "Oh my God."

Samantha anxiously scraped mud away from the text above the names of the soldiers. *What does it say?* She began using the brush end of the scraper. Her work became feverish. Finally, she laid the scraper down and leaned over as close to the tablet as possible in order to read the small type.

Samantha blew on the plaque. She brushed more dirt away, then began to read.

> *Under this stone rests a time capsule in*
> *remembrance of five Washington sons who*
> *left for war and never returned. May their souls find*
> *peace knowing that they are not forgotten.*

Deanna ran to the car. She had her camera with her and took two pictures of the stone and one of the statue. Samantha wrote down the inscriptions from both monuments.

The girls knew this was a major find. Samantha suggested they go back to city hall and ask Mr. Barker if he knew about Blocker's name being on the stone plaque.

At city hall they found Mr. Barker right where they had left him. Samantha asked, "Did you know James Blocker's name was on that stone in the park?"

"Well, young lady, yes I did. I wanted you to find it. It always seemed strange to me that he was said to never have come home and yet we were told years ago in newspapers that he died in a private hospital. Earlier I showed you the article about him being buried in 1950. Now I ask you, what's the truth? If James never came home, where was he from the end of the Civil War until 1950? Now that's what you need to find out."

Deanna was taken aback by the whole idea of what Mr. Barker might be implying.

Mr. Barker continued, "I've been the unofficial historian here in Washington for thirty years. Like you, I tried to find out things about the men on that plaque. I always ran into obstacles. No one could tell me anything. The G.A.R. records are full of holes. Those things aren't worth a damn."

Samantha asked, "What do you mean by that?"

"Look, the G.A.R. was like a club. They had rules and dues. If a member didn't go by the rules or failed to keep up his dues, they either kicked him out or suspended his membership. If you think those records are gospel, you are sadly mistaken."

"Then where did you get most of your information?"

"Ma'am, I looked everywhere I could think of. I even talked to folks in the other Washington. They seemed like they were hiding something. I got nowhere. A lot of doors were shut in my face."

"When did you ask all those questions; how many years ago?" Deanna asked.

"About twenty I'd say. I gave up."

Samantha put her hand to her chin and asked, "Why do you think Mr. Blocker here in town didn't know anything about James Blocker?"

"I don't know," replied Mr. Barker. "It's been a rumor around here for years that maybe those fellas deserted. I don't think the family, especially Miss Lillian, ever wanted to talk about it."

"My gosh," Deanna said, "We're talking about 125 years ago!"

"I know, ma'am, but families and small towns have deep secrets. I don't think Miss Lillian is gonna say much to young Robert today."

"Robert's fifty years old. Shouldn't he know something about his ancestors?"

"Perhaps so," said Barker, "but some things might be better off not shared. You know, like maybe a black spot on the family."

"That's crazy," Deanna replied. "People aren't going to hold you responsible for something someone did 125 years ago. Besides, it's only a rumor that those guys might have deserted. Is there any evidence to that rumor?"

"Well, it's been said that several people claimed to have seen some of those boys years after the war. I knew an old-timer who said he saw Blocker down near Paducah. That was when I was in my thirties. He must have seen him in the 1930s."

Deanna reeled around and said very sharply, "That's impossible. He died in 1893. You know that."

"I don't know what I know, ma'am. Like I said, you tell me what the truth is. I've heard all kinds of things over the years."

Samantha stepped forward. "Mr. Barker, you have been a world of help. I think we're going to head back to Sussex and talk to our colleagues. Mr. Blocker has my phone number. If he comes in, have him call me, please. You've really got us thinking here. I can't keep it all straight right now. Thank you again. Come on Deanna, we're heading back to see Gabe."

As they left the city hall, Deanna quickened the pace. "What the hell was all that about? Did we open a can of worms or what?"

As they approached the car, Deanna asked Samantha, "What about the guy at the hardware store. Do we want to talk to him today?"

"Not today, Deanna. I'm exhausted. I just want to get out of this town."

The girls were in deep thought as they drove to Sussex. Samantha kept catching herself driving over the speed limit. She told herself, *Slow down, slow down.*

Gabe was startled to see Samantha in the office when he returned from his noon class. "Wow, that was a quick trip."

Samantha ran to him and hugged him tightly. She didn't say a word.

"What is this?" Gabe said. "Did you have an accident or something?"

"No, I'm scared. Deanna and I had a pretty frightening morning. You won't believe what we ran into in Washington."

Gabe asked, "Where's Deanna?"

"She's at my place. She's tired and wants some time alone. I'm headed there in just a couple of minutes. Can you come over after your next class? We have to talk about this project. Some weird things are going on."

"Sure, sure, I'll be there at 4:00. Anything else?"

"Can we leave for Louisville tomorrow instead of Saturday? I think we really need time away right now."

"I'll see if I can get Marty Traub to cover for me tomorrow. He owes me one anyway. You go back to your place and pack. We'll leave tomorrow morning, okay?"

"Thank you. I love you." Samantha kissed Gabe very hard.

"...you asked me to call you if anyone asked about James Blocker? Well, two young ladies came in today and wanted information on him. I didn't tell them everything. I only showed them where the plaque was in the park."

"Was one of them named Samantha Martinson?"

"Yes, and the other one was Deanna. I didn't catch her last name."

"Very good, Mr. Barker. You did the right thing calling. We appreciate it. If they contact you again, please call. Thank you again."

♣ ♣ ♣ ♣ ♣ ♣

Chapter 8

"The secret to success is simple: do better work than any other man in your field and keep on doing it."

Wilfred A. Peterson

I couldn't wait for Friday to get here. My week was horrible. Every avenue of my research had lead to a dead end. I accomplished nothing. Marilyn and I had planned to have a relaxing dinner and perhaps take in a movie. I left the office at the university at 4:30. I liked this idea of working on my own schedule.

Marilyn got home just after 5:00. It had been a hard week for her at the bank, too.

We watched the news before getting dressed to go out. Marilyn showered and went upstairs wrapped in a towel. It was my turn. I shaved off my five o'clock shadow. When Marilyn came downstairs, she had on a black dress; the hem cut her mid-thigh. It was the latest style. I am so proud of how well she takes care of herself.

We had reservations at the Black Angus Steakhouse. Aside from Billington's, it was our favorite place. The menu options were quite different. No one made specialty steaks like the Angus. I preferred the Cajun New York Strip while Marilyn favored the Ladies Prime Rib.

At 6:00 we were ready to leave the house. Just as I reached to pull the door shut, the phone rang. "Hi, Mr. Carls, this is Deanna. We're in Louisville."

"Hi, Deanna. I thought you were heading there in the morning?"

"Well, we had a hectic week so we thought we'd leave a little early."

"Look, Deanna, Marilyn and I are just heading out to dinner. Can you call here Sunday afternoon and let me know where Samantha wants to drop you off?"

"Sure, no problem. Let me just tell you where we're staying here in Louisville. We're at the Holiday Inn East. I am in room 203. Okay?"

"Fine, Deanna. I wrote that down. If I need to get a hold of you, I'll call. Enjoy Louisville and be careful."

"Alright, Mr. Carls, have a nice dinner. I'll call you on Sunday. Bye."

As soon as she hung up the phone, Deanna joined Gabe and Samantha in the lounge. The lounge was located in a loft overlooking the inside pool.

Gabe selected a table nearest the balcony. Luckily there was a glass wall by the pool area. There were twenty elementary-age kids in the pool with their parents. The noise level must have been 200 decibels!

As Gabe looked out over the pool he commented, "Maybe we'll have a late-night swim. After bedtime for the kids." Samantha and Deanna just raised their eyebrows in agreement.

It was a quiet Friday night in the lounge: relaxing piano music, and not too busy. The nightlife in Louisville was not at the Holiday Inn.

The sunset was absolutely beautiful: a golden russet that settled over the marshes and fields to the south.

The hour in the lounge passed quickly. Gabe and Samantha promised to show Deanna the highlights of Louisville. Before they left the hotel, Gabe checked at the front desk for any messages. There were none.

Gabe drove from the hotel to Kaelin's on Newburg Road. Kaelin's lays claim to the home of the cheeseburger! Local lore says it's true. Regardless, the burgers were wonderful. Deanna enjoyed the novelty of it all. The rest of the night involved cruising "the strip" of Louisville. The night-lights showed off the sprawl of the city. Before heading back to the hotel, Gabe drove through Iroquois Park. Louisville had a lot to offer the tourist in scenic beauty.

At the hotel, Deanna wanted to retire early; it had been a long day. Even though it was only a sixty-five mile drive from Sussex to Louisville, it seemed much longer. Deanna had never been on such narrow winding roads before; especially one like Route 129 from Sussex to Vevay, which had felt like a roller-coaster ride. The drive from Vevay to Madison and then on to Louisville along the Ohio River was beautiful scenic country. The fall colors still clung to the trees.

Samantha and Gabe returned to the lounge after bidding Deanna a good night. They danced and enjoyed some much-needed time to themselves.

At 8:00 in the morning, Deanna called Gabe and Samantha's room. Samantha answered, but she wasn't really awake. "Hi, Sam. How late were you guys up?"

Samantha took a deep breath trying to wake up. "Oh, I don't know, maybe 2:00 or so."

"Wow," Deanna said, "I must have really been tired. I didn't even see 11 o'clock. I'm going to go down and have breakfast. You want me to bring you an orange juice or something?"

"No, I'll get dressed and meet you there in ten minutes, okay?"

"Sure, I'll save us a table."

Deanna sat at a table in the middle of the dining room. Samantha's ten minutes was turning into nearly thirty. Finally, Samantha and Gabe came strolling in. "Good morning, lovebirds," Deanna greeted them. "Had a rough night, did we?"

"Good morning, Deanna," Gabe replied. "The night was fine. It was the Bacardi's that were rough."

"Well, breakfast should get you going."

After breakfast the threesome ventured into the more famous shopping areas of Louisville. Bardstown Road had quite a selection of galleries, bookstores, cafés, and music venues. The same could be said of Frankfort Avenue. Gabe always enjoyed the fine foods and wines available in these quaint cafés. Their final day together was exactly what they hoped it would be.

At 2:30 Saturday afternoon they arrived back at the Holiday Inn. Check out time was 3 o'clock. After packing, they met at the front desk. To their surprise, there was a message waiting for them. It was from Mike. Gabe opened the note and read it out loud. *"Deanna, meet me at the Holiday Inn on South Route 41 in Terre Haute on Sunday. You are in room 221. I will be in room 219 if not in the lobby. See you there around noon. Mike."*

Gabe commented that Terre Haute was about an hour and a half drive from Sussex. He thought they should leave no later than 10:00 the next morning. "That will give us a little spare time, just in case," Gabe surmised.

After crossing back into Indiana, Samantha suggested they take Route 56 back through Madison. Gabe had planned to continue north on Route 65 and then cut across to North

Vernon and then to Sussex. Samantha wanted to show Deanna one last scenic wonder. Reluctantly, Gabe agreed.

Madison was a historic and charming city on the waterfront. Giant Victorian mansions lined the residential areas. The Lanier Mansion with its vast gardens had been a historical sight since the 1920s. The city itself was the epitome of historical detail. Madison was a history buff's haven!

As they came into Madison from the west, Samantha pointed left. "Turn here." The street was named Falling Rock Hill, and like other streets in this riverfront town, Falling Rock Hill was steep and winding. It was like other streets, yes, until you reach a waterfall that lurks towards your car. Local citizens declare that the water actually shoots over the road in rainy weather.

Samantha rolled her window down on the passenger side as they neared the waterfall. Although the water fell short of the road, it splashed far enough to hit the side of the car. They all got quite a kick out of the falls.

Once at the summit of Falling Rock Hill, Gabe pointed out an area where a Civil War hospital once stood. "They say some eight thousand men were treated here during the war. Many of the men were brought here directly from the battlefield at Shiloh."

The only part of the hospital complex that remained was the house where the doctors lived. In recent years it had served as a bed and breakfast.

Sussex was a short thirty miles from Madison. Deanna didn't need much time to pack. She always traveled light. They spent the afternoon at Samantha's apartment relaxing and enjoying these final hours. The concerns of the project could wait until Monday.

Samantha commented on how much she had enjoyed Deanna's stay. They had done a good deal of work and with a great deal of success. The incident at Washington was the only unresolved issue. James Blocker was a mystery. Where would they have to go to find the truth about him? The questions asked by Mr. Barker haunted them. Deanna pulled her notebook out of her bag. "Samantha," she asked, "we need to talk to Lillian Blocker. Do you think you can do that?"

"I think so. How old did they say she is, do you remember?"

"I think her grandson James said she is ninety-two years old."

"Yeah, but he also said she was mentally sharp as a tack."

"I'll call James on Monday and see if I can either talk to her on the phone or maybe set up a time to go and see her myself."

"Great, Samantha. Mr. Carls and I will be in Terre Haute all week as far as I know. You can call us there. We'll only be a couple of hours away. Maybe Mr. Carls will want to talk to her."

"That would be super. I'll let you know what I find out on Monday."

The time passed quickly. Deanna wanted to have her last meal with her friends at Marilyn's. They walked around the corner and into the small café. Deanna was brought to tears as she entered the door. Gabe had made arrangements for nearly everyone that Deanna had met in Sussex to be there to see her off. Gabe had taken care of all the details. The balloons and streamers were red and white, Oglethorpe's school colors. Deanna's chair had black and yellow balloons tied to it, Moss University colors.

Samantha gave Deanna a hug and commented, "Good thing you suggested coming here for dinner. Gabe would have killed you if you would have said Fuller's or somewhere else."

As part of the festivities, the Dean of Students at Oglethorpe, Dr. Robert Winters, presented Deanna with an honorary student ID from Oglethorpe. The ID was on a lanyard and placed ceremoniously around Deanna's neck. Deanna never felt so welcomed by a group of relative strangers. Now she truly understood what I told her about the warmth of the people in Sussex.

Marilyn had closed the café for this private party. However, as patrons came to the door, she let them in. Even people that had never met Deanna came up and wished her well. Marilyn had made sure there was plenty of food and desserts for all. The party continued until 11:00 with lively conversation backed up with good old music from the jukebox.

Gabe wanted to get up and be on the road early Sunday morning. Although he had previously suggested that they should leave no later than 10:00, he now thought earlier would be better. He called Samantha's apartment at 8:00 to see if the girls were up. Samantha answered. They had been up for a couple of hours and had even been to Marilyn's for coffee, orange juice, and toast.

Gabe told Samantha he was heading over and that they should leave by 9:00. "Why so early?" asked Samantha.

"I don't know. I just think traffic will be heavier than normal. Can you be ready?"

"We're ready now if you want to go."

"Great, I'll be right over."

Samantha hung up the phone and joined Deanna in the living room. "Well, Gabe's on his way over. He wants to leave early. He thinks the traffic will be heavy."

Deanna rolled her eyes as she replied, "He's probably right, especially around Indy. Route 465 can be a nightmare. I'm ready."

Gabe parked out in front and helped put Deanna's bags in the backseat.

The traffic was heavy on the bypass around Indianapolis. There had been an accident earlier that morning and all northbound lanes had been closed. Luckily, they had missed that. It was about 11:00 when Gabe parked at the Holiday Inn in Terre Haute. I met them at the front door. It was good to see Gabe and Samantha again, even though it had only been a week.

We discussed the string of luck they had finding four soldiers in just a matter of days. Incredible!

I bought lunch in the main dining room. Samantha and Deanna explained in detail what had taken place in Washington with James Blocker and Mr. Barker. *Strange.* I thought about what they were telling me. I tried to analyze every detail of Mr. Barker's questions. It appeared to me that he was saying something without saying it. He was dropping leads to the girls. He directed them to the park, but not specifically to the statue or the plaque on the stone. *Why?*

The statement about *"you need to find the truth"* puzzled me. I think he knows more than he's letting on. What direction does he want us to go?

I had a couple of leads on my own research, but this Blocker thing had my undivided attention.

Gabe swallowed and put down his fork. "Mike, Samantha is going to call Mr. Blocker tomorrow and see about talking to his mother, Lillian. Would you be interested in talking to her as well?"

"You bet I would. I'd also like to talk to this Barker fella. You set it up and Deanna and I will drive down. I called an old friend of mine in D.C. He's retired from the Air Force. Worked in the Pentagon for a few years at the end of his career. I asked him to look into the Arlington Cemetery situation. Let's see if he can find out anything about a no-access section of the cemetery."

As we were finishing up with lunch, Gabe asked me what I had been up to this past week. I told him that I had updated Krista Butler and the NSC on our research and how well things were progressing with our finds. I suggested that Gabe also update the NSC from his end.

We concluded our brief meeting by discussing the Internet and how helpful it had been in the project. Gabe said he would call Krista on Monday.

Gabe and Samantha were on their way back to Sussex by 2:00. Deanna and I went to our respective rooms and I asked Deanna to meet me in the main lobby in half an hour.

It only took Deanna a couple of minutes to unpack again. My Marilyn had sent some of Deanna's favorite cookies with me to give her. I had the porter put them on the desk in her room along with some fresh-cut flowers.

"Mr. Carls," Deanna called out as she came into lobby, "thank you for the cookies. What's with the flowers?"

"Don't you like them?"

"I love them, but what's the occasion?"

"I thought you deserved them for working so hard last week and for the success in finding four guys."

"Well, thank you very much." I could tell that Deanna appreciated my gesture.

"So, Deanna how was your week in Sussex?"

"It was wonderful. Like we said earlier, everyone was very helpful and we got a lot done. We had a blast as well. Louisville was fun. It was nice to just relax together and have a good time."

"What do you think of this Blocker situation?"

"Samantha and I were shocked by Mr. Barker's comments. He made it all sound so mysterious. I have to agree with you. I think he knows something too. He said it was like a big dark secret and that Miss Lillian may not want to expose something. I think it's all weird. What do you think? You're the pro here."

"Well, Deanna, I hope we get to meet with this Miss Lillian. If she can shed some light on James Blocker, that would be great. As far as Mr. Barker's comments and suggestive theories, I don't know. We'll have to see what we can find in Washington. I'd like to see those monuments you and Samantha talked about. By the way, when was that statue erected? Did you notice a date?"

"Yes, we did. I have it in my notes." Deanna rummaged through her briefcase. She pulled out a small steno pad and flipped a couple of pages.

"Here it is, 1911, May 28."

"Okay, if Miss Lillian is ninety-two years old then that means she would have been about sixteen or so at the dedication. At that age she would remember what was going on. You were told she is still mentally sharp, right?"

"Yes, both her son and Barker said that."

"Very good. We should learn a great deal from her if she's willing to talk to us. In the meantime, I have an appointment for us tomorrow to see the Vigo county clerk at the courthouse. She sounded on the phone like she may have some good additional information on the 14th Indiana Infantry. I guess years ago she was the chief county historian. What would you say to me treating you to some ice cream? I drove past a neat looking old parlor on my way into town."

"I'm up to it. Where's your car?"

I met Deanna just before 9:00 on Monday morning. Our appointment was at 10:00. We had breakfast in the hotel restaurant. Deanna had her notes on the project spread out across the table. Our list of missing soldiers was getting smaller. Both teams had been very successful. I was betting that some soldiers, possibly as many as six, would never be found. The record keeping for such a large number of veterans post Civil War was overwhelming. I don't believe the military or the government of the time was prepared for such a large task. In thinking back, it's easy to understand why such an effort by the government was needed. Each regiment kept its own records. The central government depended on the unit records to complete its own records. Thus, the final records of the government, which we are now dependent on, are only as good as the records provided to them in many cases.

The drive to the courthouse on South Third Street took only a matter of minutes. Barb Merritt's office was on the second floor. Miss Merritt was very hospitable. After our initial greeting and an explanation of our research project and its goals, Miss Merritt led us to the basement of the courthouse. The rooms in the basement were dark with no windows. The fluorescent lights were blue and seemed very bright. The room was iridescent.

Deanna's white blouse glowed, as did the white buttons on my shirt. It was an eerie feeling. I remembered this kind of lighting from my youth in arcades.

Barb told us the lighting was such that it protected archival papers from light damage. She pulled out a drawer that held papers laid out like blueprints. The writing was going to be tough to read on these old handwritten regimental records. She told us that there were records here from four regiments from Vigo County. Our job was made a bit easier because the 14th was the only infantry regiment. Two of the regiments were artillery and one was cavalry.

"If you two are alright here, I have to be back upstairs. There's a phone on the table over there if you need me. Just pick it up and dial 288. Call me when you're ready to come upstairs. I have to lock the door behind me so don't panic; it's policy. Here are some white gloves for you to handle the documents. I know you'll be careful. I hope you find what you need."

"Thank you, Miss Merritt."

Deanna put on a pair of gloves as she bent over the documents in the drawer. The old fragile pages had turned dark brown in color. "Cool," she said as she looked up at me standing next to her. The whites of her eyes beamed in the blue light.

Civil War regimental records are extremely detailed. The regimental quartermasters listed everything from the issuing of socks, to wounds received in battle, to the shipping of bodies home in metal coffins. Everything was there. He noted when soldiers were ill and even when they had visitors in camp. Deanna and I were certain we could find good information here.

Deanna took the list of soldiers from her pocket. She scrolled her finger down the left column looking for any reference to these names. On the third page she stopped and then moved her finger slowly to the right.

"Here's one!" she exclaimed. "Norman Kinnder, Private, Co. A. I think on our list we have his name spelled KINDER. Maybe that's why we haven't found anything before."

"I don't think so, Deanna. Our search would have found him either way. Read what it says about him. Anything there?"

"It says he . . .owed the quartermaster for two blankets, one pair of heavy socks, writing paper, one ink well, two pens, one muslin shirt (red), and three dollars he borrowed on January 11."

"I am very impressed. The quartermaster really kept great records."

"Listen, it goes on. It says . . .Kinnder was wounded in the leg at Antietam on the 17th of September 1863. Leg amputated on the 21st. He was left in a hospital in Sharpsburg, Maryland, for three weeks and then transferred to an army hospital in Ohio. That's all it says about him."

"I guess we'll have to ask Miss Merritt if they have any tax records or death certificate for him after the war. Maybe he came back here to Vigo County. See if you can identify any other names."

Deanna scrolled down each page. The lighting most certainly protected the pages, but it also made it nearly impossible to read the entries. Every so often Deanna would pause and try to figure out what the exact words were. She turned each page very slowly and with great care.

Deanna had just turned the page and began her usual scrolling movement when suddenly she stopped and began to chuckle under her breath. There was the page containing the information I had long looked for. "Here's our boy, Thomas Overland, Private, Co. I."

I butted in and wanted to read this entry myself. Thomas Overland. Wonderful! Here it was, the official firsthand account of Wes and Mary's long lost relative: the man with the gold watch.

I had to see what the quartermaster of Company I had written. *Deducted from his pay, $17.41 for materials purchased from Jan. 1 to May 27, 1862 and $11.56 for materials purchased from June 11 to Dec. 14, 1862. Suffered bullet wound to right shoulder at Winchester, March 23, in hospital ten days, returned to duty Apr. 15. Complained of foot infection and removed from active duty for two weeks June 1862. Shot in chest (mortal) May 9, 1864 at Spotsylvania, Left in Army Hospital #161 near Cold Harbor.*

"Mr. Carls, we know he didn't die in 1864. His wound wasn't mortal."

"I know, Deanna, but the quartermaster wrote what he thought was true. They left him behind. He thought he was dying in the hospital. Most chest wounds at that time were fatal. If this is the last we here of Overland in the regimental records, no wonder nothing else shows up. You can't discharge or pay a pension to a dead man."

"What do you think happened?"

"If there is nothing else, I assume he recovered and just went home on his own. The war was winding down, so maybe he just left."

"What about the watch he received in 1871?"

"I was thinking about that. I don't know what to say; maybe he just appeared out of the woodwork. Perhaps we can find some newspaper articles on the tenth reunion where he received the watch. Why don't you plan on looking into that? Try the state library here in Terre Haute. They have a large microfilm collection; maybe you'll get lucky.

"Okay, I'll do that this afternoon."

We looked at the remainder of the reports. There were no further listings or mentions of the other soldiers on our list. Deanna gingerly closed the books and slid the drawer back into the cabinet. Our work here was completed.

I called extension 288 and Miss Merritt answered. "Are you finished down there?" she asked.

"Yes, ma'am, we are." I answered.

"I'll be right there. Give me a minute or two."

As Barb escorted us out, I thanked Barb for all her help. The material we found here would be of great value to our research. It never ceased to amaze me how cooperative library archivists are. They do a wonderful job and are usually not given the credit they deserve.

On the way back to the Holiday Inn, I told Deanna about my friend Jason Leathers in Washington. Jason was going to look into the situation at Arlington National Cemetery. Knowing Jason, he would do a thorough job for us. He had a good many contacts in Washington. Washington was a city full of secrets. If it's a really good secret, we'll hear about it soon enough. There's always a whistle-blower!

Deanna called the state library branch in Terre Haute. The archivist gave Deanna his undivided attention. Deanna asked for information on the 1871 reunion of the 14th Indiana Volunteer Infantry. We were interested in where the event was held and if there were any articles or records concerning who and how many veterans were in attendance. The archivist said he needed a couple of days to gather what information they might have.

I contacted the county clerks in the surrounding counties and inquired as to their records of any of the remaining soldiers. My gut feeling was that my search wasn't going to yield any results. I don't know why, it just didn't feel good.

On Wednesday morning I was paged from the front desk of the hotel. Deanna was swimming and I was taking some down time to read in the lobby. I was enjoying my coffee and the peaceful midweek day.

"Dr. Carls, Dr. Michael Carls," the front-desk clerk called out.

"Yes, here I am," I responded.

"Urgent message for you, sir," he said as he handed me a hand-written message.

The paper was folded in half and stapled. I pulled the paper open, tearing it slightly at the staple. I read the words in silence:

> *Call Samantha or Gabe IMMEDIATELY.*
> *Concerning Gene Fife.* 10:14 a.m.

I hurried to the indoor pool and found Deanna talking with other hotel guests on the far end.

"Deanna, come here. Quickly!"

"What is it?"

I handed the note to Deanna. She read it and asked, "Is it a heart attack?"

"I don't know. I'm calling Gabe. If it's that serious, we're leaving right away. Why don't you dry off and get dressed just in case."

I took the elevator and got to my room as fast as I could. I had Gabe's number written on the very top of my notepad. I really should have it memorized by this time.

Samantha answered the phone on the first ring. "Hi, Mike, thanks for calling so fast. Gene Fife had a stroke at 9:30 this morning. He was at work when it happened. Dorothy called us right away. Apparently Gene told her to call. They took him by ambulance from Vevay to Madison. She's at the hospital in Madison with him now. What do you think we should do?"

I thought for a moment about what Samantha had said. "Can you or Gabe get there this morning?"

"Yes, I can leave now if I have to."

"Good, you do that. I'll get Deanna and we'll head to Sussex. Call us at your office about 1:30. We should be there by then."

"Okay, Mr. Carls, and I am sorry I called you Mike. I never do that."

"It's alright, Samantha. That's my name, just use it."

"I'll take just a couple of minutes here and tell Gabe I'm going to Madison. He'll be waiting for you and Deanna. Have a safe drive and don't worry. I'll see you guys later."

"Very good, Samantha. We'll leave here real soon. Say hi to Dorothy and tell her we're praying for Gene. Bye now."

Deanna and I packed our bags and went to the front desk to check out. The clerk knew we were leaving for an emergency.

I told him we might be back to finish our work in Terre Haute and also asked him to take any calls coming from the county clerks I had talked to. He said he would and wished us well on our drive.

I called Gabe to see if he wanted us to pick him up in Sussex. He suggested we drive straight through and that he would join us in the morning. I called Marilyn at the bank and told her what had happened. She was very concerned. Marilyn had never met Gene, but she had heard a great deal about him from me.

Samantha made the drive to Madison in about thirty-five minutes. Gene was being taken care of at The King's Daughter's Hospital. The hospital has been around since 1899 and serves as a regional facility. Dorothy was alone in the waiting room. She was elated to see Samantha, who gave her a huge hug.

"Oh, Miss Martinson," Dorothy sighed, "thank you so much for coming."

The doctor came out to talk to Dorothy just before noon. "Mrs. Fife, your husband is resting. It's too early to say for sure, but I don't think he'll have any permanent physical losses. The next two or three hours are critical. Do you have someone here with you?"

"Yes I do. This is Samantha Martinson from Sussex. She's a family friend."

"You can come back and see him for a minute. He's sleeping, but he can hear you. Just tell him you're here. You might want to get some lunch and relax. Gene is in good hands and he's stable for now. You should be able to stay with him in a couple of hours. Alright?"

Samantha took Dorothy's hand as they followed the doctor down the hall. Samantha commented on the beautiful facility.

As they entered Gene's room, Dorothy began to cry. She had never seen Gene like this in a hospital. Gene was fast asleep. He had two IV's and a breathing pump. The telemetry monitor flickered. The screen showed the ups and downs of the heart's rhythm and blood pressure. Gene's blood pressure at this time was 102 over 72. Everything that could be done was being done. All Samantha and Dorothy could do was wait.

"Thank you, doctor," Samantha said. "We'll get some lunch just down the street. I'll have Mrs. Fife back in a couple of hours."

Dorothy leaned over the bedside and kissed Gene on the forehead. In a soft voice that echoed her age, Dorothy uttered, "I love you."

Deanna and I kept up with traffic on the 465 Bypass around Indianapolis. We were making good time. At this rate we would be in Sussex about 1:30 or so.

I told Deanna I guessed Gene's age to be around seventy-four or five. Deanna agreed but commented that he had a lot of energy for someone that age. It certainly was true that Gene enjoyed working. He wasn't one for sitting at home doing nothing. Gene was very involved in our project. He was making calls to his friends and colleagues all over the state trying to help us locate our soldiers. We greatly appreciated his work. It was only right that we be there for him.

The traffic thinned out about twenty miles south of Indianapolis. I figured the fastest route Madison. At Columbus, I cut across Route 7. This was a direct shot to Madison. I thought it would be about forty-five miles from that point.

Meanwhile, Samantha and Dorothy were having lunch at the Key West Shrimp House on Ferry Street. Although they were several blocks from the hospital, it was only minutes away. Having Samantha there was a godsend for Dorothy. Dorothy let her mind drift and enjoyed the view of the Ohio River and the barges passing by.

Dorothy told Samantha that she and Gene often came there to eat with their boys back in the seventies. It was one of her favorite places and it held fond memories. Dorothy went on about the boys throwing a football in the open field just outside the restaurant's west windows. The large, grassy area in front of the neighboring President Madison Motel made a wonderful playground.

"Deanna," Dorothy asked, "did you know that this building used to be a pearl button factory? Look at the old handmade beams inside here. The original commission is still here too."

"No, you're kidding?"

"Yep, the young people used to go right out into the river and stir up clam shells with pitchforks and then scoop them up in nets. They would bring them in the building here and drill out ten or twelve buttons from each shell. They had a special machine to drill the four holes in the middle. Young girls would sew the buttons on cardboard squares and that's what we'd buy at the store. A little history for you."

"That's pretty neat, Dorothy," Samantha replied. "I had no idea."

"Oh honey, that was many years ago. I was quite young back then."

Samantha was glad Dorothy had picked this particular restaurant for lunch, which obviously meant a lot to her. At this time, it was good to have such memories. Their waiter, Scott, was very attentive and had a good sense of humor. Samantha commented later that he was one of the most gracious hosts she had ever encountered.

Deanna took the road map out of my glove box. As she opened it she asked if Samantha had mentioned what street the hospital was on. I told her that Samantha said we should take Route 7 straight into Madison and that the hospital was at the bottom of the hill. She said we couldn't miss it.

We arrived in Madison at 1:45. I parked in the lot to the south of the main entrance. As Deanna and I exited the car, Samantha and Dorothy were pulling in just a few cars from us. We greeted Dorothy with warm hugs. I asked, "How's Gene doing?"

Samantha said they were just returning from lunch, but that Gene had been resting when they left.

I thought Dorothy was doing well considering what was going on. We all walked into the hospital together and settled into the waiting room.

Dr. Brunner came to see Dorothy at 2 o'clock. He seemed very young to me. The older I get, the younger fellow teachers and colleagues appear. The doctor said Gene was still resting and that all his vital signs were good. We were all relieved to hear that.

I asked Dorothy if Gene's work might have been responsible for the stroke. Had he been upset, or maybe overworked? It was then that she told us what happened at work that morning. Samantha and Deanna sat on the edge of their chairs as Dorothy related to us a conversation she had had with Gene just an hour before the police called her.

Gene had called Dorothy at home shortly after he arrived at work. He had received a phone call from Krista Butler. Dorothy said he was very upset. Dorothy then said that Gene was going to call me today to discuss Krista.

"Did he tell you what Krista said to him that made him so upset?"

"No, he said he'd talk to me later about it."

"Okay, Dorothy, I'll call Krista and find out why she needed to talk to Gene. I can't think of any reason for her to call him."

Samantha and Deanna were equally as baffled.

I went to my car and grabbed my briefcase. I had Krista's number in my planner, used the phone in the hospital lobby, and made a third-party billing call to the NSC.

Krista answered the phone and was quite surprised to hear my voice. "Dr. Carls, how nice to hear from you again so soon."

"Miss Butler," I said rather harshly, "what on earth did you need to talk to Gene Fife about this morning? The man was so upset he had a stroke."

Krista was silent. Then in a tone that seemed genuine, she said, "Oh my God, how is he?"

"We don't know how he is right now. He hasn't come to yet. He's resting. Again, what did you need to talk to him about?"

"Dr. Carls, I'm so sorry. I was just following up on your progress with NSC. I assure you, I didn't mean to upset Mr. Fife. I feel awful. Is there anything I or the NSC can do?"

"Yes, there is, as a matter of fact. Tell me why you're so damn interested in our project? I called you last week and updated you on all our finds and the Internet use. Why did you need to call Gene? I have to tell you, I'm really getting suspicious of your real intentions."

"Dr. Carls, I don't know what else to say. I can only tell you that I have been assigned to oversee your project."

"Well, that isn't good enough. What's really going on here? You make me think I have to be watching by back every minute. Who else have you called? Are you calling every county clerk in the counties I told you we were looking into? Are you?"

"I can't answer that."

"What do you mean you CAN'T answer that? You better answer that."

"Dr. Carls, I have to go. Tell Mrs. Fife I'm sorry that Mr. Fife got upset and I wish him the best. I have to hang up now."

The phone went dead.

Well, I'll be damned! I was in a rage. What was I going to tell the girls and Dorothy about this? I thought about it for a minute. I decided not to say anything at this time. I would talk to them later, maybe after dinner or at a motel if we stayed overnight.

Just as I entered the waiting room, Dorothy and the girls were going in to see Gene. I joined them. Dorothy insisted we all accompany her.

Gene was awake but a bit drowsy. Dorothy again kissed his forehead. He had given us a real scare. It was apparent from his facial gestures that Gene wanted to say something, but the words weren't coming out at the moment. He needed to rest. We told him we'd stay overnight and see him in the morning. Dr. Brunner felt that Gene would be able to talk to us by tomorrow.

We left the hospital around 4:00. Dorothy wanted to take all of us out for dinner but I wouldn't here of it. Dorothy had called their sons and told them about Gene. Jake, the middle son, lives in Cincinnati and would be in Madison later this evening. The other boys had called the hospital, but couldn't make it home right away. Dorothy told them she'd keep them posted on their father's progress.

Dorothy insisted we spend the night here at her house. "There is plenty of room. No need for you folks to waste money. I won't take no for an answer." We had no say in the matter. Dorothy felt perfectly comfortable being twenty miles away from the hospital.

Jake arrived with his wife, Barbara at, 5:30. Dorothy told them they could go see Gene after supper if they wanted to. Visiting hours ended at 8:30. We all introduced ourselves to Jake and Barbara. Jake took my hand and said, "Thank you very much for being here with Mom. I've heard a great deal about you and your project from Dad. He really enjoys the research. It makes him feel like he's part of something important. I think he needs that."

"No problem, Jake. We're glad we found your father. He's been a real help to us. Plus, like you say, he enjoys it. It shows. I hope it's just not too much for him."

I still hadn't told Deanna or Samantha about my conversation with Krista. I had to wait for the right time when we would be alone.

Jake and Barbara wanted to go to Madison as soon as possible but before they left, Jake offered to buy dinner for all of us. He called a local restaurant in Vevay and ordered carryout. I thanked him on behalf of all of us and prepared to pick up the food in forty-five minutes. Jake and Barbara left for Madison immediately after dinner, around 7:00.

I asked Dorothy if she'd be all right if I took Samantha and Deanna with me to pick up dinner. I thought she might want some time alone. She said, "My Lord, you go right ahead. I'm not going anywhere." The girls looked at me wondering why I wanted them to come along.

Once in the car, I told them what Krista had to say. Samantha was particularly enraged. "I knew it from the beginning. I don't like that woman and I don't trust her."

Deanna had the same sentiments. My question to them was, "What do we do now?"

Samantha thought we may want to call all the county clerks we've dealt with and ask them if Krista or anyone from the NSC has contacted them. I wasn't quite sure if we should take a direct approach like that. Deanna didn't say anything at first.

Finally, Deanna offered a different plan. "Why don't we play the Krista game. Let's do things just as we have been, keeping

149

her up to date with what we're doing and stuff. But, let's plant some fake leads out there and see if it gets back to her. That way we can control the flow of information."

Samantha and I both laughed at the simplicity of Deanna's thinking. It was very sixth-gradish, but it would probably work. The girls began an animated dialog conniving their plan. In the meantime, I was driving and looking for the restaurant.

I awoke the next morning to the smell of sizzling sausage. Dorothy was up and cooking breakfast. There was nothing that gets to my heart faster than a freshly brewed pot of coffee. Dorothy's spirits seemed noticeably lighter as she bummed around in the kitchen. It was 8:15 and the girls were still asleep.

Dorothy said she had called the hospital at 8:00 and the doctor told her Gene had slept through the night and was showing good signs. His blood pressure was slightly higher and he had good color. We were all planning to visit Gene midmorning.

I was sitting at the table enjoying a cup of Dorothy's coffee when Jake and Barbara came in the side door. "Good morning, how's everyone doing today?" Jake greeted.

I held up my mug and said, "Couldn't do better than this."

Jake said they stayed in Madison last evening. Gene was talking some last night just before they left. He said he wanted to talk to me today about Krista. Barbara said he was weak, but appeared mentally alert. Barbara also commented that Gene complained about a numb feeling in his right arm. The doctor was concerned, but told them not to be too worried about it just yet.

We visited for a while and then decided to wake the two princesses so they wouldn't miss breakfast.

After breakfast we all drove to Madison. I rode with Jake while the ladies followed in my car. It gave me a chance to talk to Jake about what was involved in our project and exactly what his father was doing for us. I felt it necessary to tell him a little bit about Krista Butler and the NSC. I had to be careful not to say too much.

Jake was thankful for my sharing the information. I assured him I would confront Krista. I also apologized for our group in case this was in any way the cause of his father's stroke.

As we entered the hospital, I spotted Gabe standing by the gift shop door. He had just arrived from Sussex moments before us. I shook his hand and told him we needed to talk. He hadn't been in to see Gene yet, but that time would come soon enough.

Deanna, Samantha, Gabe, and I stayed in the waiting room while Dorothy and Jake went in to see Gene. Barbara, who is an LPN in Cincinnati, was talking to the nurses on duty at their station who were sharing as much information as they could. In just a matter of minutes Barbara joined Jake and Dorothy.

Jake came out and said Gene wanted to talk to Samantha and me, alone. As we entered the room, I was relieved to see Gene sitting up. I took that as a good sign despite the IV and oxygen tube. He looked very tired.

Samantha gave Gene a gentle hug. Gene's response was appreciable. He said he had slept most of the night. Gene stared at me and said he had something very important to share with the two of us.

As he leaned forward, I stuffed a pillow behind his back. He breathed a sigh of relief. "The other day I had a call from that Krista person. She got me so damn mad. I figure that's why I'm here. She kept asking me all kinds of questions about where you guys are looking for information and who you all talked to. It was like the third degree. I couldn't get her to shut up."

"Gene," I said, "don't worry about any of that. I've talked to her already and I'll be talking to her again real soon. You just worry about Gene. Try to put all that out of your head for now."

"It's not that easy. She mentioned my boys and having her friends look into them...you know, IRS and such."

"Okay, Gene, I get the picture. Just relax. I've had enough of this. I'm calling her immediately. That sounds like a threat."

"You bet it's a threat. That's just how she put it too."

Samantha was noticeably upset. She patted Gene's hand and kissed his forehead. I excused myself from the room. In the waiting room I told Deanna to go on in and join Samantha. I motioned for Gabe and Jake to join me in the hallway.

"Jake, I am so sorry. Your dad just told me about his phone call with Krista Butler. That's what got him so stressed out. I can't imagine what she could be thinking, scaring a man Gene's age. I have to call her NOW. There's a phone in the cafeteria. I have my credit card. I'll be there if you need me. I have to find out what she's up to."

"Mike, don't blame yourself. Dad's a big boy; he wouldn't have gotten involved with you and your project if he didn't want to. I don't blame you for his stroke. His clock was ticking and it just happened. I'll go to the cafeteria with you and get coffees for the ladies."

"Thanks, Jake, I appreciate your understanding. I think Gene will be okay. He seemed pretty sharp, don't you think?"

"Yes, I thought he looked much better. I was expecting worse."

"By the way, Deanna only takes OJ and toast in the mornings."

I waved Jake off with my left hand as I completed dialing with my right. Gabe sat next to me while I made the call. The receptionist at the NSC answered. I asked for Krista Butler's extension. There was a lengthy wait. The phone rang several times to no avail. Finally, the operator came back on the line. "I'm sorry, sir, there is no answer at that extension."

"Fine, can you page her?"

"Yes, sir, I can do that. Please hold."

After two or three minutes the operator came back on.

"Sir, Miss Butler is in a meeting all morning. Can I have her return your call when she's available?"

"By all means. This is urgent. You tell her that. Tell her its Dr. Mike Carls from Moss University."

I gave her the number at the hospital, thinking that we would be there at least until noon.

We joined the others in the waiting room. Barbara and the girls were having quite an animated conversation. Dorothy was in with Gene. Jake stood as I came in, looking like he needed a walk. We walked outside the hospital. The temperature was dropping. It must have been near thirty degrees.

"Well, Mike, did you talk to Miss Butler?"

"No, she's in a meeting all morning. I left my number here. I said it was urgent, so maybe she'll break away and call sooner."

"Look, Mike, I talked to the doctor while you were downstairs. He said dad's stroke was minor; it shouldn't leave any permanent damage. He just has to take it easy for a few weeks and then cut down his part-time hours if he wants to work."

Gabe interjected, "That's good news. Anything we can do to help out your mother?"

"No, Barb is going to stay with them the rest of the week. Dad can go home tomorrow afternoon after some blood test results come back. He'll have some meds, but he needs to rest and stay off his feet for a while. I have to get back to the office and clean up a few things anyway. I'll be back here on Thursday."

"Okay. We'll stick around here the rest of the day and then Deanna and I'll get back to Terre Haute. We have some research on hold there. Again Jake, I can't tell you how sorry I am about this whole thing."

"Like I said before, nonsense, it's not your fault. Barb and I are glad you're here. Dad appreciates it too. I know he does. Mom thinks the world of you guys. I think she wants to adopt Deanna and Samantha, the daughters she never had."

I called Marilyn to let her know about Gene. She was equally relieved to hear that there was no permanent loss. I told her Deanna and I were heading back to Terre Haute to complete our research and that we should be home early Friday afternoon. Gabe and Samantha were probably going to stay later than us, but they were only thirty to thirty-five minutes away in case they needed to come back.

Gene was resting soundly after lunch. Deanna and I made plans to return to Terre Haute. After saying our good-byes, I asked Jake to call the Holiday Inn in Terre Haute if there was any change in Gene's condition.

Gene was in good hands. Gabe and Samantha walked us out to my car. Gabe had to get back to Oglethorpe for classes in the morning, so they would not be staying much longer either. Samantha had more leads to follow up on as well. I had called the Holiday Inn to make sure they had a couple of rooms for Deanna and I. Not a problem on a Tuesday night.

Deanna was rather somber on the drive back to Terre Haute. I think the seriousness of what could have happened was setting in. We talked about Krista and the NSC. Over the past year we had given Krista numerous updates about the project. Why then is it that all of a sudden she is so curious about the details of our research? She had said several times that the subject of our research was not the issue, but how we were using the Internet. I was now convinced that the opposite was true. Of the twenty-three missing soldiers, we had found sufficient information to close the case on nearly fourteen. We were very near closure on another one or two. I felt that our efforts were decidedly successful. The Internet websites had proved to be extremely valuable. The system was working. The NSC could be proud of what they had accomplished. At least that was my thought anyway.

Deanna went to the front desk to get our room assignments as I parked the car and grabbed our bags. The front-desk clerk had three messages for us. One was from Marilyn, wanting me to call home as soon as possible, but not urgent. The other two messages were from county clerks in Parke County and Vermillion County. Deanna was especially pleased that they returned her call. Perhaps they had some positive information for us.

I called Marilyn as soon as I checked into my room. She just wanted to tell me that Joanne Darling had called and told her the interview with Jim Brackett had gone well. She was almost certain that he would be joining the research staff. I thought that would be a good addition based on what Samantha and Deanna had told me about him.

While I was talking to Marilyn, Deanna made return calls to both Vermillion and Parke counties. The only information she could get was from Parke County. They had old tax records indicating that Thomas Overland had rented farm property just north of Rockville and just south of Bloomingdale.

The clerk told Deanna that Overland had resided in the county for eleven years, from 1869 to 1880. Records indicated that he had moved to the area from Baltimore. Overland sold his dairy business and relocated sometime after 1880. Because there are no additional tax or death records, we can only assume that he moved out of the county. All in all this was wonderful news for us. We now had confirmation that

Overland did survive the war and that he was in the area for the tenth reunion.

Overland must have stayed in the East after he recovered from his wounds. It is probable that he was transferred to a larger hospital in Baltimore based on the extent of his wounds.

The clerk in Vermillion County had no information for us on any of the names we provided. I thought for sure there would be something, considering the county's proximity to Terre Haute, the home of the 14th Indiana Infantry. However, we reveled in locating Overland.

We continued to call and visit the surrounding counties and local historical societies. It seemed as if our luck had run out. Nothing. The clerks and volunteers at the courthouses and museums were very cordial. I believe they did their best at finding any information. Perhaps we were coming to the end of the road.

After dinner on Thursday, I called Samantha's apartment. Gabe answered the phone. They had just gotten in from Madison. Gabe said Gene was resting just fine. Dorothy was holding up and enjoying the time with Jake and Barbara. Gabe and Samantha were both exhausted. I told Gabe about Overland. I also told him we seemed to have hit a brick wall with our last five soldiers.

Deanna and I would return to Sycamore on Friday, probably earlier than we had planned. Deanna wanted to scout out the small towns in east-central Illinois on our drive back. She and Marilyn would be planning a small search of the area just in case any of our soldiers had lived there.

Although our research in Terre Haute had not lived up to my expectations, it was done. The secrets of the missing soldiers had to be found elsewhere. I really wanted to meet with Mr. Barker in Washington, but that would have to wait. Gene Fife was a dear friend and his wellbeing was a much higher priority. The soldiers on my list have been missing for 125 years; they could wait a little longer.

Chapter 9

"Success seems to be largely a matter of hanging on after others have let go."

William Feather

Marilyn came to my office around 10:00. We were going to go over a map for her and Deanna to plan their trip. Deanna was on an errand for me at the library. Marilyn hadn't come to the office in quite some time and as she looked around, she seemed to approve of the décor; it wasn't fancy by any means. The constant hum of the computer mainframe seemed to bother her, however.

At Deanna's cubicle, Marilyn looked over the pictures pinned to the cloth-covered dividers. "Cute. Nice picture of Deanna and Samantha in Madison. They certainly get along well, don't they?"

"Yes, they do."

Deanna had a purple Troll with yellow hair sitting on top of her computer. Its name was "Virus." I explained to Marilyn what a computer virus was. It made sense to her then. Deanna was one to have cute, little things on her desk.

I introduced Marilyn to Jim Brackett, who Joanne had hired shortly after our return from Terre Haute. Jim and Marilyn hit it off from the start. They had similar personalities. Jim was originally from the East Coast and his family still lived in the Boston area. Jim asked Marilyn for some decorating ideas for his work area. I just shook my head. The bank environment of Marilyn's was a far cry from that of a research lab.

Deanna came in just as Marilyn was focusing on Jim's cubicle. "Oh no, don't tell me he has you decorating the place." Deanna chimed in, shaking her head too.

"Well," said Jim, "someone has to bring this place into the twentieth century. Look around here. It's all plain colors with putty-colored, plastic computers and desks. Yuk!"

Marilyn got a chuckle out of Jim. Who would have thought a young guy like Jim would be so concerned about style and color? Marilyn suggested a few live plants and maybe a couple of paintings on the outer walls; anything to jazz the place up a bit.

As we ventured back to my desk and the map, Jim followed along. Marilyn carefully looked at the map. "I've never been there, or there, or there. It's all new territory for me."

Deanna placed her index finger on the map and let it flow over the countryside. She was thinking all the time. Then she said, "I estimate it to be about a three-hour drive. We can hit all the towns in that area in two or three days. I've already called the city halls in Paris, Charleston, Mattoon, and Effingham. I suppose we'll need to do the same for Champaign and Urbana."

Marilyn was in agreement. She knew it would take more time, but they also needed to look in Cook County and in the Kankakee area as well.

Finally, we all sat down and planned in detail the schedule for their research. Deanna and Marilyn would concentrate their efforts down state while operating out of Champaign. I would take the area around Kankakee, north of Rantoul, but south of Chicago. It was a large area on the map, but few towns were included. We decided to do as much of the research over the phone as possible. Winter was upon us and driving conditions could be pretty bad. Deanna would solicit the phone numbers. Marilyn had the week before Christmas off from work. She would make as many calls as possible. Deanna would do likewise in between other research projects with Dr. Darling.

Dr. Brackett was still getting himself orientated to Moss. He hadn't requested any research yet, but his day was coming. Deanna would be very much involved along with David Hinman. To be honest, Deanna would probably not have any free time between Christmas and spring. The winter months were always the busiest for research requests.

Now that everyone had their assignments, I offered to break up the meeting and suggested lunch. However, I only invited Marilyn. She and I hadn't had a private lunch out together for some time. Today was the day. I had already made reservations for us at a small off-campus pub. The food was rumored to be very good. I knew the atmosphere was a bit dark, but very romantic. Besides, Deanna had recommended it to me.

I gave Deanna a voucher from our grant money to buy lunch for Jim, David, and her. They were going to Billington's. Good choice.

It was a joy to be alone with Marilyn. I missed her terribly while I was in Madison and Terre Haute. We talked about her upcoming research with Deanna and the drive and time away from home. It would only be a couple of days, but still some time away. I could see that she was looking forward to it. Not necessarily the being away, but the involvement; doing something different, exciting. She had so enjoyed the meeting in Indianapolis last fall. For me, I was ready to work away in my little cubicle all winter.

After lunch, I returned to the office. Marilyn had the rest of the day to herself. She wanted to shop a little and then go home and just rest. Take a nap. The older I get, the more of those I enjoy too.

I called Gabe at Oglethorpe. He and Samantha were planning on checking the counties of northern Kentucky around Louisville. They had several events going on at the college. The research would have to follow our plan here, and wait until spring. Samantha would make calls to the county clerks and any other historical societies or museums in the area. Her approach was identical to Deanna's.

Gabe and I talked for some time. He had followed up on our discussion of Krista Butler. He called her and made a routine update of our activity since Gene's stroke. He said she inquired about Gene's health, but didn't bring up anything about why she had called him that day. Gabe didn't ask, either. Gabe mentioned to Krista that Samantha would be calling the county officials in Bullitt and Spencer Counties in Kentucky this week. He didn't say any more. We had decided to follow Deanna and Samantha's plan and feed Krista only the information we wanted her to have.

At one point, Gabe said Krista was concerned about our feelings toward her. She emphasized that she could be trusted and that she was interested in our research and how the Internet was working for us. Gabe's attitude was agreeable, but he was still wary of her real intentions. He said it was a cordial conversation. After what happened to Gene, I don't know if I could have pulled that off so soon.

After hanging up with Gabe, I called Dorothy Fife. Dorothy was just great. She said Gene was much improved and resting, as ordered by the doctors. She also commented on Gene's eagerness to get back to work. "When he's up to it . . . he can only work a few hours a week for some time."

I was glad to hear of Gene's progress. Dorothy was such a peach!

Marilyn called and said a letter came from the NSC. I told her to go ahead and open it and read it to me over the phone.

I could hear her tearing the envelope. I heard her take a breath.

"What is it?" I asked into the phone.

"It's from Krista Butler. She wants to meet with you in January. She says she has to talk to you in person. She'll be in Chicago on the fifteenth and sixteenth for a conference. She enclosed her home address and phone number and she wants you to call her in advance so you can schedule where to meet.

I was in shock. I would finally get to meet the person behind the voice. I must have really upset her. I asked Marilyn for Krista's phone number. I thought for a minute and then decided to call her from home tonight.

"Mike, what do you think she wants to talk to you about?" Marilyn wondered.

"I don't really know. We do have a sizeable grant from NSC. Maybe she has some new Internet information to share with us. What I do know is that you're going in with me to meet her. That's for sure."

"That's fine, I don't want you in there alone with her anyway. I mean, I trust you and all, but she seems manipulative."

"Thanks, hun, but I mean I need you there to hear what she has to say. I always think two heads are better than one. I'll call her at home tonight and set up the meeting. Isn't there a nice little Italian place on North Clark Street that we went to a couple of times? See if you can remember the name and give them a call. Let's plan on a late afternoon dinner meeting. She should be able to get away from her conference by then. If it's not possible, we'll find out tonight. I better go for now. I'll see you in a couple of hours."

I couldn't wait until Deanna returned from lunch. I wanted to see her face when I told her about Krista.

I didn't have to wait very long. Deanna, Jim, and David got to the office at 2:00. I gave Deanna a huge smile. She knew something was up.

"What's up, Mr. Carls?" she asked.

"You are not going to believe it. Krista Butler sent me a letter requesting a meeting next month. She'll be at a conference in Chicago and she wants to get together."

"Good," said Deanna, "I'd like to meet the little bitch. I'll tell her what I think of her for causing Gene's stroke."

"Whoa, Deanna, we're not just going to barge in on her and beat her up. I'm taking Marilyn with me and we're going to listen to what she has to say."

"You mean I'm not going to meet her?"

"That's right. Not now. Not the way you're feeling about her. Let me check out the situation. I don't know what she wants, but Marilyn will be there too."

Deanna was pouting; being left out hurt her. I let her brew in her cubicle.

My heart was racing as I dialed Krista's home phone number. It was 7:30 her time, so she should be home from work. Krista answered with a hurried voice. "Hello."

"Miss Butler, this is Michael Carls."

"Mr. Carls, thank you for calling so quickly. I hope we can meet in Chicago."

"Yes, we can. That's why I'm calling. My wife, Marilyn, and I can meet you on the evening of the fifteenth. Is that okay with your schedule?"

"Yes, fine. Do you know the area?"

"Yes. We thought you might like Italian. On North Clark Street there's a small bistro called Caesar's. It's very nice and quiet. I think you'll like it."

"That sounds just great. I am very anxious to meet you and your wife. I have some important things to talk to you about. I am very upset with the Gene Fife situation. I want to clear the air, if you know what I mean."

"No, I don't really know what you mean at all. Perhaps we can clear up a lot of things on the fifteenth."

"I'm sure we can. I'm really looking forward to meeting you. Let's say we meet at 7:30 the evening of the fifteenth. I think my last meeting lets out at 5:00. I'll take a cab to Caesar's. Sorry, but I have to run. My date is picking me up for a late dinner tonight. You know how it is in D.C., everyone out here eats late."

"Miss Butler, we'll see you next month. Thanks for getting in touch with me. I, too, am looking forward to meeting you. Have a good dinner and good night."

"Well," I told Marilyn, "that wasn't so bad. We're all set on the fifteenth at Caesar's. She sounded perfectly innocent to me. Let's see what she has to say then."

I immediately called Gabe and Samantha and told them I would be meeting with Krista in Chicago on the fifteenth of January. They were both somewhat surprised. They were mostly surprised because I told them that she was the one who initiated the meeting.

Samantha informed me that she wanted to go ahead with her search in the Louisville area. I encouraged her to wait until spring, but she insisted. She had some distant family in the area and wanted to visit them as well, so I certainly wasn't going to tell her no, don't do your research.

The rest of the team was settled in for the upcoming winter and Christmas season. Deanna had the additional task of helping Jim Brackett getting orientated to our department.

Requests for research were coming from various departments. Jim Brackett had his first assignment at Moss. I believe it had something to do with vascular transplants or heart something. All I knew was that it was way over my head.

Joanne Darling had a few small projects for Deanna. One project required her to go to Northwestern University in Evanston, Illinois. I suggested she take Jim Brackett along and Deanna was agreeable to that. David Hinman was still working on his search into East African cultures.

I sat in my cubicle and wondered what to do next. I thought about charting our progress. Somehow seeing things in three dimensions makes them easier to understand.

I took an old corkboard on wheels from the storage area and cleaned it up. What a dusty mess. The chalkboard on the reverse side was black and cracked. I used pushpins to diagram our team and typed the names of the veterans on small pieces of paper. Next, I divided them up according to whose team they were assigned to. I used string to indicate where each of the identified vets lived. The picture before me was becoming clearer and clearer.

Not surprisingly, the web that surfaced focused on central and south-central Indiana. We had other links that might take our research to northern Kentucky, but that was the exception. Marilyn and Deanna had good reason to look in central Illinois, but that appeared to be the last area of real concern.

As I looked at my work, the mail came in. I had a manila envelope from the state library in Terre Haute. The contents of the envelope made my spirits quickly fade. I thought we were doing so well. I had asked one of the archivists to do a bit of research for me into the G.A.R. records.

According to his research, the G.A.R. hit its highest membership number of Union veterans in 1890. That year, their membership reached its peak at 408,489. The Union army officially listed 2,675,000 men as having served in the Civil War. If that's correct, fewer than 20 percent of the veterans were G.A.R. members. Also, according to his research, Albert Woolson of Duluth, Minnesota, was the last Union veteran and G.A.R. member to die. He died on August 2, 1956, at the age of 109.

I guess I had put too much faith in the G.A.R. records to find all our answers. How foolish of me. I should have known better. My Civil War research experience had been in the area of battles and military organization. Personal histories were not my forte prior to this project. I knew it would be difficult. Now I knew it would be almost impossible. Yes, there were other Civil War veteran organizations, but I have no idea where to locate their records or how to determine their accuracy.

I didn't want to spoil everyone's holiday season so I put the material away in the bottom drawer of my desk. I would share it with Gabe and the girls at some future time. For now, I'd see what I could find.

When I arrived at home that day, Marilyn sensed my low spirits. She asked me immediately, "What's wrong?" I'm not very good at hiding my emotions.

"Oh, nothing."

"Don't nothing me, Mike Carls. I know you better than that."

I didn't want to tell her about the G.A.R. files. She was really looking forward to her travels with Deanna in the spring.

"Marilyn," I said, "I hit a small stumbling block on our research today, that's all. Nothing to be concerned about."

"Michael, I don't believe that for one minute."

"Okay. It might be bigger than a small block."

"Do you want to talk about it?"

"Not really. I think it'll be okay. Besides, we have a meeting with Krista. Maybe I can run this by her and see what she has to say."

"You really think she's going to help you?"

"I don't know. It may be a last resort."

"Well, you sound awful doomy and gloomy."

"I'm sorry. I don't want to spoil your evening. Let's talk about something else, like what's on T.V."

"Better yet, why don't you go watch the news while I make dinner?"

Marilyn knew that food would put me in a better mood. I had to force myself to not throw in the towel. I had good colleagues and they knew what they were doing. Being their leader, I had to keep my chin up.

Marilyn and I sat in the dining room and had a delicious meal. I swear that woman can cook anything from scratch. We were just about finished eating when the phone rang. It was Jason Leathers in Washington, D.C.

"Hello, Mike?"

"Yes, this is Mike Carls. Is this Jason?"

"Yeah, how are you? I got the lowdown for you on that Arlington stuff you asked about."

"Really? Let's hear it."

"You told me your guy was buried in Section 244, Block 11, right?"

"Yes, I think that's right. I don't have my notes in front of me right now."

"That's okay. I looked over there yesterday. Me and the misses just kind of strolled around a bit, ya' know? Anyway, there is no Section 244. There's a Section 44 way back in the corner. It's on all the tourist maps, but there's nothing back there to draw people. They all want to see the Kennedy's and the changing of the guard. Anyway, we go strolling and I find this section. I start looking around, like you asked. I see this here headstone with your guy Blocker's name on it. Well, what's really weird is that I see four other stones just like his, ya' know, new and such. I wrote down the names for ya'."

"Jason, are you sure about this?"

"You bet your ass I'm sure. A couple of Ft. Meyers guys ran us out of there. I told them we were just walking the cemetery. You know, playing tourists. Anyway, I wrote down the names of the other soldiers. You what those names too?"

"Sure, Jason, who are they?"

"Oh, before I get to the names, the headstones were a little different than the normal Civil War ones. These stones only had the name of the soldier and the state he was from. At the top of each stone it says 1861-1865. No mention of company or regiment. Strange, huh. Okay, here are the names I got: Jacob Winslow, Indiana; Micah Pandarri, Indiana; Thomas Caldwell, Indiana; and Charles Dix, also from Indiana."

"You are not going to believe this, Jason. All four of those men are on my list of missing. That's incredible. How can I explain that?"

"I don't know, man. It all sounds pretty weird to me. Were these guys all involved in the same action or something?"

"Some were and some weren't. I am completely baffled. I don't know what to say."

"Well, Mike, there you have it. I hope you can solve this thing you're researching. Let me know what you find out, okay?"

"Sure, Jason. Thanks again for going to all the trouble. I really appreciate it. I owe you one."

As I hung up the phone, Marilyn was quick to ask what that was all about.

I sat still for a moment pondering what to say. I handed her the piece of paper that I wrote the names on. She read them and asked me if these were some of our missing guys.

"Marilyn," I said, "they are all on our list."

Marilyn looked down at me as I sat in the overstuffed chair. "How can that be?" she asked. "There have to be some records somewhere on these guys. Why haven't you or Gabe found them?"

"I don't know. I simply don't know. This brings to light more questions for Miss Butler. Remember, she told Gabe the government didn't want anyone back in that section of the cemetery. She has to know something."

I decided not to call Krista and start asking questions. I'd wait until January to see what see had to say.

I called Gabe the next day and told him about Jason's find. Gabe was stunned. He thought they had some good leads on Caldwell and Dix. This revelation changed everything. Gabe said Samantha was determined to continue looking in the Louisville area. I suggested that Gabe not share this new information with Samantha at this time. I would do the same here at Moss with Deanna.

December brought cold weather and long nights. It was hard to believe that it had been a year since Wes first gave me Gabe's article. We had come so far. Now, like a novelist, we had hit the proverbial brick wall in our research. Samantha couldn't seem to find any information in Louisville and Deanna was tied up on other projects. I hadn't the same enthusiasm since my conversation with Jason. I just couldn't get into it.

I spent my Christmas time off from school reading and relaxing. Marilyn kept things going around the house. She was always envious of my school holidays and vacations. Her work at the bank was constant.

We had a good Christmas with friends and family. The nights in front of the fireplace were most relaxing. We hadn't used the fireplace as much as we thought we would when we first bought the house. This year it seemed more inviting and worth the extra work. Now would be a good time to relax and rethink the project. We knew that we would have to develop new paths for our research. The challenge would be exciting.

Chapter 10

"If we value the pursuit of knowledge, we must be free to follow wherever that search may lead us . . ."

Adlai Stevenson

The January snows hit hard. Our campus was closed for the first three days of the second semester. The holiday season had come and gone and the students were back at Moss. I looked forward to my first spring semester of not doing Joanne Darling's legwork. In years past she always had plenty for me to do in the spring.

David Hinman and Deanna would be busy. I had a couple of weeks to put things together before my meeting with Krista. The mainframes were in need of constant monitoring. The system was growing so fast. The media and technical updates from the National Science Commission were coming in daily. The newest system advancement was to be called the World Wide Web, or WWW.

Although I was technically on leave from the school, I tried to keep abreast of things. The day of going back to work was fast approaching. I had heard a lot of scuttlebutt about what might be happening with the Internet system. To me it sounded like science fiction.

On the tenth, Samantha called just to touch base. She hadn't had any luck locating any information while she was in Kentucky. She went so far as to say that the people she talked with seemed a little closemouthed. It didn't surprise me. After all, she was in the heart of Dixie inquiring about Union veterans! The people of the South still had a burning desire for and dedication to their forefather's cause. I suppose I'd feel the same way if I had gone through the Reconstruction period. Those were brutal years for the South.

Gabe was back teaching. Samantha was continuing to teach part-time in the social studies department. I talked about the NSC memos concerning Internet development and what they might mean to us in the future. The entire research area was about to change. From what I could ascertain from articles in magazines and in the news, changes wouldn't be too many years away. For a researcher, these were exciting times.

Marilyn left work early on the fifteenth. We had a small lunch before our drive to the city. I never could judge the flow of traffic on the East-West Tollway. Once I reached the Naperville toll plaza, the traffic became much more congested. I thought it would take us just over an hour to get to Clark Street.

Near the Hinsdale oasis things got really bad. Even though it was only 2:30 on a Friday afternoon, it seemed like rush hour to me. I wasn't used to this kind of traffic. Marilyn must have told me a thousand times to never move her into this area. The area was fine, it's the congestion that's the problem.

I missed my turnoff on State Street downtown. But Chicago is a very forgiving city. I knew that I could still get to where I wanted to be if I remained patient. Sure enough, it was only a matter of blocks before I was on the right track again.

Since we were so close to the area we needed to be in, we decided to park the car and take in a little sightseeing. We walked pass the Downtown Hilton Hotel. I told Marilyn that this was where Krista's meeting was being held. Marilyn wanted to go in and look around. *Fine*, I thought, *I didn't mind looking at the lobby and stuff, but I wasn't going to page Krista or anything like that.* As I said to Marilyn, "I wouldn't know her even if she stood right in front of my face."

We still had a little time to kill, so we stopped at a small café only a block or two from Caesar's where we each had a cup of coffee. As I sat there I was trying to visualize what Krista might look like. I knew from our conversations that she was relatively young. Aside from that, I had no idea. Marilyn had taken so well to Deanna and Samantha, I wondered how she'd do with Krista.

At 6 o'clock I was ready to head over to Caesar's but Marilyn thought it was a bit too early. I hate to while away time. I always misjudge times when I came to the city. You just never know what might cause a delay or something. Marilyn and I kept on talking and taking up space in the café. The owner didn't seem to mind. He said his dinner crowd wouldn't be in until 6:30 or so. I was beginning to think Chicago must be a lot like Washington, D.C. insofar as eating late dinners.

Finally, we left and walked to Caesar's. We arrived just a few minutes before 7:00. The maitre d' showed us to our table even though we were early. I ordered drinks as we waited anxiously to meet Krista.

At 7:20, a very attractive, tall, thin, professionally dressed, blonde stood next to the maitre d' podium. She was looking over the crowd in the restaurant. Marilyn didn't think that she could be Krista. She just didn't think so. As we watched, the maitre d' led the young lady our direction. They stopped next to the table. I stood to introduce myself. "Miss Butler, I assume?"

"Dr. Carls, I presume?"

"Yes, and this is my wife, Marilyn."

"Pleased to meet you, Mrs. Carls."

"Nice to finally meet you, Miss Butler. I've heard a great deal about you."

"I'm sure you have."

Krista sat down across from me and to Marilyn's left.

I could tell she was a bit nervous, but then all of us were. I signaled for a waiter and I ordered a beverage for Krista. We exchanged small talk about the January weather and the sights and sounds of the city. I was going to let Krista get to the heart of the conversation since she was the one who requested the meeting.

We ate our dinner as we began to discuss our project and our fellow team members. The conversation was basically general in nature. At one point, Krista bent over and took a standard number ten–size envelope out of her purse. Without breaking stride in her discourse, she handed it to Marilyn and told her to put it in her purse. Calmly, Krista instructed Marilyn, "Please open this later, after I leave."

Marilyn was taken aback by Krista's request. At first she simply did as Krista requested. But curiosity got the best of her. "What's this about?" Marilyn asked.

"Mrs. Carls, I can't go into detail with you right now. The contents are self-explanatory. I know you both have a thousand questions for me about the NSC and our interest in your research. I can, however, update you on the changes you'll see with the Internet. Officially, that is the purpose of this meeting. What's in the envelope is something I can't discuss. All I will tell you, off the record, is that it will help you with your project. Please don't ask me to explain. My bosses know I'm meeting you here in Chicago, but only to update you as an Internet development site. Do you understand?"

"Of course," I said.

"Good. I have some papers here for you to take back to Moss. Since you are listed as the program contact person, I have to personally hand this to you. I have to do the same at the other four sites."

Krista handed me a small stack of papers—probably fifteen to twenty sheets. While I glanced quickly through the papers, Krista and Marilyn started up a cordial conversation. I could hear them discussing something about living in D.C. and being in the heat of things; sort of like life in the fast lane.

As I perused the information, I was amazed at what I was Amazed at what I was reading. It was as if science fiction was becoming science faction! I knew things where happening with the Internet, but I had no idea how fast. No one was making up this stuff; this was an official communiqué from the NSC.

According to the NSC, in 1986 there were approximately 50,000 hosts and hookups to the Internet. These hosts were primarily government agencies, universities, and specified research labs. The NSC anticipated that number to surpass 300,000 by the end of 1989. In addition, there was a new development called "browser/editor" which would allow users greater access to documentation. This may not sound very dramatic, but to anyone used to the hassle of getting documents previously, this was a major leap forward. The next area of development would be the improvement of the browser so that access could be gained through the click of the computer mouse.

I understood the facts and figures presented in the report but still had no idea of a time frame for their activation. I didn't have to wait very long to get that answer.

Krista looked at me and asked, "What do you think?"

"I'm amazed at how far the system has developed. It sounds wonderful, but what do you see as a time frame for full implementation?"

Krista smiled and then offered an answer. "Dr. Carls, that's why I'm here and that's why I have watched your project so closely. What you read in the report goes live in less than one year, possibly as soon as six months. The whole system will be opened for public use no later than eighteen months from now."

"That's great news, Miss Butler."

"Yes, it is great news. But it also raises a number of concerns. The government originally developed the Internet system, as we know it, for military use. They were very good. I'm sure that there are avenues that they don't want the public to view or have access to. The question of regulating the system comes into play. Who plays God in other words?"

"So yes, it's a good thing to develop. Now, how do we manage it?"

Marilyn and I pondered Krista's statement. We certainly had no suggestions. I was still looking forward to the changes to come. I guess that was the researcher in me. I saw many uses for material and information gathering. I could see my job getting easier and faster.

Krista went on. "There are a number of sensitive documents that, by law, have to be made public. The people in Washington are really up in arms about the freedom of information laws. When they passed that law, the documents were out of reach to the general public. Not any more. The law says that the public must have full access. You can bet that there are people in Washington right now scrambling to hide records before this plan goes live."

"So, why are you telling us this?" I asked.

"Because, Dr. Carls, your project is right smack in the middle of it."

"What . . . how?"

"I can't say any more than that. Open the envelope later and enjoy. Please believe me. I took a real chance with my career here tonight. Let's have a good dinner and some time together.

I am on your side. I think you are good people and I know you work hard. You have a genuine love of research and it shows. You're persistent. That's good. The NSC has taken notice of you. I'm sure that if you should request a grant in the future there will be no objection. You do understand?"

"I think I do, why is it so important that we not open the envelope now?"

"What envelope is that, Dr. Carls?"

Now I truly understood. Whatever was in the envelope was directly related to our research and was not to be discussed. Krista was telling me that if I go along in silence, future grants were assured. Fine.

I turned toward Krista and asked her, "So, Miss Butler, what college did you attend?"

From there, our conversation and the rest of the evening was more relaxed. Krista was a charming young lady. Marilyn enjoyed her company immensely.

We concluded our dinner meeting around 9:45. Krista insisted on taking a cab the few blocks to the Hilton. I shook her hand with sincerity. I could see in her eyes that she had a compassionate soul. Marilyn gave Krista a hug and suggested that she consider coming to Sycamore for a site visit. Krista was open to her suggestion and thought next summer would be a good time for that.

Marilyn and I stood there as Krista's cab pulled away from the curb. We each waved. I looked at my watch and asked Marilyn if she minded spending the night in the city. She agreed. It would be quite late by the time we drove home. We were both tired.

Not far from Caesar's was the Windward Inn. I checked with the front-desk clerk as to the availability of a room for the evening. We were in luck. They had three rooms left. Our room was on the seventeenth floor with a magnificent view of the city.

We had no luggage and no change of clothes since we hadn't planned on spending the night in the city. This was a first for both Marilyn and myself.

As we entered our room, I began a self-guided tour. Marilyn sat on the sofa and opened her purse. "Aren't you interested in reading what's in the envelope?"

I walked back into the living-room area and paused, looking at Marilyn, "I don't know if I'm ready for what's inside. I don't know if it's good or bad. I guess there's only one way to find out. Go ahead and open it up." I sat next to Marilyn on the sofa.

Carefully Marilyn tore the top of the envelope open. Inside were three typed pages on standard white paper. Marilyn began to read:

> *Dr. Carls,*
>
> *As you read this, I want you to keep in mind that I am sincerely sorry for any anguish that my actions in the past may have caused you or your colleagues. I am especially sorry for Mr. Fife's situation.*

Krista went on about our research and how it had helped the advancement of the Internet use and the NSC's understanding of the system as a whole.

Then her letter continued:

> *As I mentioned to you, you are persistent. Eventually you'll find most of the men on your list. It was no accident that your project request was granted. The NSC was quite surprised when your request came in. As you know, the NSC is involved with a wide variety of projects and you stumbled on to one of them.*

Do you remember our conversation about Arlington Cemetery? I certainly do. You were getting very close. There is a section of the cemetery, Section 44, that is offlimits to the general public. If you look there, you'll find five markers on Block 11. All five of these men are on your list from Indiana. That part of all this is purely coincidental. I will tell you that these men had no immediate families that the NSC knew of at the time. It was only later through your research that we found out otherwise. I will also tell you that ALL these men died after 1950.

I know, you're asking me how that is possible. The records list their deaths between 1893 and 1910. Believe me, they didn't die before 1950.

Krista continued by explaining the project's original goals and reasoning.

Medical science had advanced to a stage that it was felt that certain drugs and treatments may help older persons handle various illnesses. The doctors of the time were confident that their efforts were medically sound and well within moral parameters.

Krista's notes went on:

The shocking part of what I have told you thus far is that the project began in 1917. Hard to believe, isn't it? I had a hard time believing it too. The project's name was Unit Blue. I guess they picked that name because all the men were Union veterans. Clever.

The NSC, through me, did contact county clerks in a number of counties in Indiana and Kentucky. I told them to either not provide you with information or limit what information they gave you. In one case, you were given misleading information to delay your efforts. Tell Miss Martinson I'm sorry for that. I was being watched to make sure I complied with orders.

I tell you all this now because of the system's rapid development. It's only a matter of time before all this is available through the Freedom of Information Act. I thought by telling you ahead of time, you can save yourself and your colleagues a great deal of work.

Krista's note concluded:

I know that the medical portion of the 1917 experiment has concluded. I believe that there are two veterans on your list that you might find records on. They were not part of the program, but I found their names mentioned in a file here in our offices.

I believe if you research the far western counties of Kentucky you will find closure information. A while ago I talked to a Judy North in Wingo, Kentucky. You will want to contact her.

I only ask that the medical experiment program remain confidential. Please cover for me here. I thought you needed to know. I wish you the best in completing your project. If I can help in any additional way, please let me know. I will no longer be involved in deterring your efforts.

Thank you for understanding.

Krista Butler

Marilyn handed the letter to me. "Wow, that's an eye-opener," she exclaimed.

I reread some of the lines. "Medical experiments. Can you believe it, back in 1917?" My mind was racing. Even though I was tired, sleep was almost impossible. Marilyn and I talked for a long time before either of us fell asleep.

Of course, Krista had no idea that I already knew about Section 44 at Arlington. I had to believe her. Marilyn and I both thought she was very sincere. We had located Blocker's family, but the others were still on our to-do list.

Once we returned to Sycamore, I'd call Gabe or Samantha and try to act as if everything with the project was normal. If I was going to share any of Krista's information, it would be with Gabe. This entire project originated through his efforts. He had a right to know.

Marilyn agreed with my thinking. She still wanted to spend some time with Deanna in central Illinois next spring. I wasn't going to deny her that. Marilyn thought there was still more work to be done. Her concern was that the other four men buried at Arlington might also have family that the NSC missed. After all, they missed Blocker's family.

For the next couple months we rested on our laurels at Moss as well as at Oglethorpe.

Chapter 11

"Dreams that do come true can be as unsettling as those that don't."

Brett Butler

It was wonderful to feel the warmth of spring approaching. The winter months had been exceptionally hard. I can't remember a colder winter. My age must be catching up to me.

Over the months, Marilyn and Deanna had made their plans to continue their search. Marilyn had spread her maps on the coffee table many times. She highlighted the routes they'd take and the towns they'd visit. It was a big adventure for her. The trip had been planned for several days over spring break in early April.

Meanwhile, I had made plans with Samantha to visit Washington, Indiana, and possibly meet with Robert Blocker and his grandmother, Lillian. Samantha handled the arrangements. Our trip was planned to coincide with Deanna and Marilyn's.

I was curious about what the NSC must have told the Blocker family back in 1911 when the plaque was dedicated in the park. I remember Deanna had telling me that Lillian was sixteen years old at the time. Knowing what I now know about James Blocker, I was more determined than ever to meet Miss Lillian.

The school days finally ground down to spring break. Thank goodness. It's always a long haul from January to spring break. I don't think students realize that the faculty also needs a break.

Marilyn had been packing all week. She made arrangements with her aunt in Champaign to operate out of her house on Hollycrest Street. They figured they might have to motel-it one night. Deanna was going to do all the driving since she finally had her convertible up and running and Marilyn consented. They planned on leaving early Saturday morning.

My plans were to leave for Washington at almost the same time. I was going to meet Samantha at a rest area on Route 65, east of Washington. Samantha had reservations for us at a motel in town. I had a 370-mile drive; Samantha was only sixty miles away.

Deanna arrived at our house just after breakfast, around 7:00. Marilyn was excited and anxious to get going. I helped Marilyn load her bags in the trunk. After a kiss and a hug they were on their way. It was a beautiful April morning. I figured they would wait until the sun had been up a little longer before the top went down.

I took my time getting things into my car. It must have been about 9:15 before I pulled out of Sycamore. I had told Samantha to start looking for me at 4:00. I brought along a few new cassettes to play in the car. Marilyn had bought me a new one cassette with several of my favorite tunes. It was just me and my car heading back to southern Indiana again.

By noon I was just west of the Indiana state line near Danville, Illinois, pulling into a rest stop. I called Samantha. I told her I was making good time and would probably be earlier than 4:00. She said she had talked to Robert Blocker and that we would be having dinner with him around 6:00. Great!

In the meantime, Deanna and Marilyn made it to Champaign and Marilyn's aunt's house. Aunt Ida lived alone and would certainly enjoy the company. If I know Marilyn, she had already planned on doing something special to thank Ida— perhaps a meal out or a day of shopping.

Samantha was at our meeting place right on time. I followed her into Washington. We would be staying at the Cantigny Suites Hotel. Actually, the name was a misrepresentation of the rooms. Nice, but not that nice.

Samantha's room was down the hall from mine and directly across the hall from the indoor pool. Since we had better than two hours before dinner, she decided on an afternoon swim. I grabbed a book and joined her at the pool. This was a nice, relaxing way to start what turned out to be an extremely hard week.

I called Mr. Blocker at 5:45 and told him that we would pick him up in just a few minutes. He said he would be ready. Samantha remembered how to get to his house on North Cross Street. The white, wood-framed, ranch-style house was identical to most of the neighborhood homes. Robert was standing outside as we parked at the curb.

Robert was a large cordial man. I would guess him to be six-feet five-inches tall and most likely around 245 pounds: a big man. He certainly towered over Samantha and me.

We were having dinner at the Palmer House Restaurant just outside of town. Robert knew the owners very well and had requested a quiet table so we could talk.

Samantha and I told Robert what we knew about James Blocker. I did not share the information that I had learned from Krista Butler. Robert was very interested in learning more about this lost relative and was amazed that he had been kept in the dark for so many years. He promised us his full cooperation. He told us that he had talked to his grandmother and that she would meet with us at noon the next day.

Samantha and I were a bit surprised that Miss Lillian would be willing to talk after all these years. Robert said she was very agreeable to the meeting and to discussing James. Lillian lived in a care facility so Robert would pick her up.

We met Robert and Lillian at the YMCA for lunch. The dining room overlooked the river, just above a small waterfall. The view was just beautiful in the spring. Lillian sat staring out the window as we arrived. Robert stood as we approached the table.

"Grandmother, these are the people I was telling you about. This is Dr. Carls from Illinois. And this is Samantha Martinson from Oglethorpe College in Sussex."

Lillian turned toward us and in a very quiet voice uttered, "Pleased to meet you folks. I hear you want to know about my grandfather James."

"Well, Miss Lillian, we can talk about that later. How are you? I hear you're having a birthday soon, is that right?"

"Oh yes, I suppose so. I don't do much celebrating anymore. I'll be ninety-three on the twenty-first. Too many candles for me."

Samantha leaned over toward Lillian and commented, "Well you certainly don't show your age. I hope I look as good as you do if I live so long."

"Oh honey," Lillian said with a smile, "you don't want to live this long. It's pretty lonely. Most of my friends and acquaintances are all gone now. I have Robert here, but he doesn't want to hang around an old lady like me."

Robert took Lillian's hand and said, "Now Grandma, you know I love you for your looks. You're still my favorite girl."

"Nonsense," replied Lillian, "you don't need to waste your time around an old woman like me."

As we were eating, Samantha asked Lillian if we might ask her a few questions about James. Quaintly, she replied, "Now deary, let's not try to think when we're supposed to be eating. It's hard for the mouth to chew and talk at the same time."

After lunch, the four of us took a short stroll to the benches that line the shoreline by the dam. We sat there in a row with Lillian in the middle. Lillian looked at Samantha and said, "Now, what is it that you want this old woman to tell you?"

"Lillian, do you remember the day the statue in the park was dedicated? You would have been about sixteen years old at the time."

"Yes, yes, I do remember that day. It was a rainy day. Warm, but rainy. I remember my father was there with a black umbrella. All the men back then wore black suits every day. Times were different. There were people there from all over the county, lots of people. Most of them still had horses, but I think there might have been a couple of cars there too.

Samantha asked if there was a tribute or any remarks made about her grandfather. Lillian looked at Robert. Robert held the old lady's hand. She was quivering slightly.

"Robert, I always wanted to tell you about your great-grandfather, but I just couldn't. I guess it's okay now though. At the time of the statue dedication, everyone thought your great-grandfather was a deserter. One day in camp he just disappeared. That was the story. The military told us he was missing. Some old soldiers said they saw him all over the place. Some folks said they saw him in Texas. My mother never believed them though. She knew James too well. Over the years the stories died out and, except for me, the people did too."

Again Samantha asked Lillian, "What happened in 1950 when you heard that James was being buried in Arlington National Cemetery?"

"That was very confusing to us. By that time, mother had died and I was grown with my own family. They told me that they moved grandfather's body from somewhere to that Arlington place. I can't remember from where. I never went there to see his grave or anything. I remember that it was in all the papers and such. Some folks tried to make a big deal about it. I just decided then and there that I'd not say anymore about it. All I knew was the rumor about grandfather being a deserter. It was embarrassing. That's why I never said anything to you, Robert. I guess now you have a right to know. These folks here can find out more. The truth always comes out in the end."

"Miss Lillian, may I ask you one more question?" Samantha requested as she put one hand on Lillian's shoulder.

"Of course, hun," said Lillian.

"Do you ever remember hearing anything about James dying in a private hospital in like 1893 or so?"

"No, not at all."

"Over the years, Miss Lillian, has anyone ever tried to talk to you about James before? You know, like maybe a writer or a researcher, someone like that?"

"Oh, let's see. I think it was just a year or two after the time they told us about the Arlington thing; a young man called at the house and asked a few questions. He wanted to know about grandfather's Civil War battles or something along those lines. I don't remember what he wanted for sure. Never heard from him again though."

"Miss Lillian, do you know any of the other men whose names are on the plaque in the park?"

"I didn't know them, but I knew some of their families here in Washington. They're all gone now. There's no one left from those days."

I was taking notes as fast as I could. Lillian was indeed very sharp. She had told us more already than I expected. I had a couple of questions myself, but they could wait. Lillian looked tired. It was an emotional time for her. The family secret was out. It didn't matter anymore. Robert certainly wasn't upset about it. Lillian was from a different age, a different time. Society had changed. It was almost the 1990s. Families aren't families like they once were. Everything is different.

We sat there on the bench for what seemed to be several minutes of peaceful solace. The rush of the water over the dam was soothing. All was quiet. The birds in the shrubs were busy making nests for soon-to-be laid eggs. The gentle, spring breeze was a breath of freshness.

Lillian sat forward on the bench and turned toward Robert, asking, "Do you have a black footlocker that was your mother's?"

Robert thought for moment and replied, "Yes, I think so, in the attic. Why do you ask?"

"I believe there's a letter in there that I gave your mother many years ago. It was from grandfather. I remember thinking that maybe she would want it. It's an old letter. There might be an envelope with it. Yes, I know I gave it to her."

We all sat there, stunned. Out of the blue Lillian remembered this letter. Wonderful! Robert thought it was time to get Lillian home. She liked to relax and nap in the afternoons. Robert suggested that we go to his house while he took Lillian back to the senior center.

Samantha and I sat in the car and waited for Robert. We couldn't believe our luck. We were eager to see if the letter still existed and what it said. We thought Lillian had proved to be a goldmine of information. We were astonished by sharp memory.

Robert turned into his driveway and motioned for us to follow him into the house. He pulled down the ceiling ladder that led to the attic. All three of us climbed up. The roofline was such that we couldn't stand upright. Bent over, we maneuvered to the back corner. There it was—the footlocker! Robert told us his mother had been killed in an auto accident when he was nineteen. The locker had been in his parents' house until his father passed away two years ago. Pulling the locker out of the corner, Robert said, "I just assumed this was old photos and newspaper clippings. I never went through it very thoroughly. After Dad died, I had to clean out the house. It sold pretty fast."

Robert insisted we haul the locker downstairs. The attic was a bit warm. I helped him lug it down. We placed it on the floor in the enclosed back porch. The breeze felt good after being in the attic.

Inside the locker were hundreds of old family pictures just as Robert suspected. There were also old auto policies, little league newspaper clippings, a homeowner's insurance policy, and countless receipts. Near the bottom of the locker I found a small stack of envelopes tied together. They appeared to be holiday cards and birthday cards. Robert said to go ahead and untie them and look through them.

I gently untied the string. There were about thirty envelopes and cards. As I separated them, I saw the envelope from James Blocker. I looked at Samantha and said, "Here it is." I handed the envelope to Robert. It was his and he should open it.

Robert took the frail, brown page out of the envelope. The paper was crisp and I thought for sure it would tear when he unfolded it. Samantha and I have handled hundreds of old papers like this. Robert's big hands fumbled with the paper. He handed the empty envelope to me. I noticed that there was no return address, only a postal mark. The mark was faded, but I could still make out some of it. It said KENTUCKY, May 11, 1903. I was fairly certain it was 1903. The 19 and the 3 were very clear.

Robert read what he could from the letter. It had been written in pencil and was very washed out.

May 11, 1903

Mother,

I am fine. I have been＿＿＿＿＿for a few mon＿＿. I can no＿ write to yo＿ for they tell me that I m＿st not. They are t＿king goo＿ care of us here.

One of the ho＿＿tal workers w＿＿l get this to you. I will tr＿ to write a＿＿in soon.

Give m＿ love to al＿

Your obedie＿t son,

James

Robert sat silently for a minute and then asked, "I thought you said he died in a hospital in 1893."

"Yes, Robert, that's what the records say, 1893, not 1903."

"And Robert, the letter was mailed from Kentucky. Look at the stamp. James says a worker mailed it for him. It sounds like he was being held in a hospital and no one was supposed to know he was there."

"Strange," said Samantha. "We've seen these kinds of things before. This scenario has a bit of a different twist though. We'll have to keep looking until we can figure it out."

I just looked at Robert and Samantha. I knew that there was more to this story, a lot more. I kept remembering what Krista had told Marilyn and me in the letter. I would try to keep it secret as long as possible.

We looked through the locker for any additional letters and we found an envelope that was similar to the other one, but there was no letter inside it. The envelope was stamped KENTUCKY, but the date was completely worn away. Robert kept the letter and the two envelopes aside. The three of us visited for the remainder of the afternoon. Later Samantha and I would return to the motel and compose our notes and try to put the puzzle of James Blocker together.

I returned to my room to find the red light blinking on the phone, indicating that I had a message. I called the front desk. The message was to call Marilyn at her aunt's house later tonight.

Samantha and I met in a small side lounge next to the pool. It was a glass-enclosed room with tables, overstuffed chairs, sofas, and a T.V. We took a table and began sorting through our notes. We attempted to draw some kind of chart connecting the 14th Indiana to Blocker, to various battles, to Block 244 (really 44) in Arlington, to a private hospital in 1893, to Kentucky in 1903, to a plaque dedicated in 1911, and to reburial in 1950. This puzzle had a lot of missing pieces. Our research raised more questions than it answered. Our talents as researchers were being put to the test.

After dinner at the hotel, I returned Marilyn's call. She told me that she and Deanna had a nice visit with Aunt Ida and that they had called around to various towns in the area. Tomorrow they were going to Effingham, Illinois, to talk to a man at the historical society. They think he may have information on Frederick Gale. I was surprised indeed. We had found nothing on him so far.

I asked Marilyn, "What makes this guy think he has something on Gale?"

"Well, when Deanna made the call, she mentioned a few names that we were interested in. For some reason, Mr. Brown in Effingham jumped on Gale. He said he did research on local Civil War veterans in Cole County years ago and that he remembered the name. We're going to check it out tomorrow."

"That's wonderful, Marilyn. You struck gold on your first time out."

"Thank you, but Deanna's the one who found him."

"See what you can find out. I'm curious about how and when he ended up in Illinois."

We talked awhile longer about how things were going. Deanna was thrilled with the information from Lillian. I told Deanna to drive carefully.

Marilyn and Deanna left for Effingham, about fifty miles southeast of Champaign, around 8:00. They were to have breakfast with Aunt Ida and planned on meeting Mr. Brown shortly after 9:00. The drive was pleasant. The warm sun and gentle breeze was very refreshing. Marilyn was having the time of her life. She was really looking forward to getting in on a find.

In Effingham, Deanna parked in front of the old railroad depot that housed the historical society. Marilyn thought the building closely resembled the depot in Madison, Indiana. Both buildings were now historical societies.

Theodore Brown was the head volunteer at the center and he had volunteered there since the society's inception in 1982. He was also the author of the county's history and brochures on its participation in the Civil War. I guess one could call him the authority on Cole County history.

Deanna cut right to the chase. She asked Mr. Brown what information he had on Frederick Gale. Accustomed to such requests, Mr. Brown had already pulled what information he had and handed it to Deanna. She sat at a table in the center of the room and opened the file. Marilyn joined her at the table while Mr. Brown looked over her shoulder.

"There," said Mr. Brown, "in that picture is Frederick Gale. Third from the right."

The picture was taken in 1923. The county had hosted a Fourth of July festival to honor all Civil War veterans. In the picture were seventeen men. Each man's name was written above his head. Two of the men in the picture had no names identifying them.

Deanna continued looking through the papers in the file. There was an old newspaper article. The article must have accompanied the picture. There were brief descriptions of each veteran. Marilyn read the article aloud.

Of the seventeen men, four were from Indiana. Frederick Gale was said to be from southern Indiana and to have served in the 14th Infantry, Company K. This was most certainly our guy!

Mr. Brown went on to tell Deanna and Marilyn that he had heard Gale was a farm implement dealer. Then Mr. Brown flabbergasted the girls with one final tidbit. "Would you like to see where Mr. Gale is buried?"

Deanna replied, "You have that information too? You bet we want to see his grave. What else can you tell us about him?"

"Let's just walk across the street," said Brown.

There was an empty lot across the street from the depot. Deanna and Marilyn looked at Mr. Brown. Marilyn asked, "What's supposed to be here?"

"Over there in the corner," Brown ordered as he pointed.

In the far corner of the lot was a flat grave marker nearly covered with grass. It said there were forty-one graves in the lot. This at one time was the county potter's field.

Mr. Brown went on to explain that Frederick Gale had gone bankrupt and died penniless in the county home. As far as the records were concerned, Gale died around the time of the stock market crash, 1929. Mr. Brown had no idea why Gale wasn't listed as discharged or why he was passed over for a pension.

Mr. Brown said that he had heard that Gale had a family, but that they all left the area when he went broke. The old man was left there alone, so the county took him in. There was no documentation to back up the story. I suppose it doesn't really matter. We now knew where another old soldier rests.

Marilyn told Deanna she couldn't wait to tell me about Gale. She was liking this work. After a relaxing lunch with Mr. Brown in Effingham, they were on their way back to Champaign.

The rest of the week for Marilyn and Deanna was uneventful. There were no more leads. Pure luck had produced the information on Frederick Gale.

Deanna made a few calls to the Chicago area. She had several contacts that might be of assistance and gave them six names to work with. She told her friends that she would be in touch with them in a week or so once she returned to Moss.

For the meantime, Deanna, Marilyn, and Aunt Ida spent several hours a day and most evenings enjoying her solarium on the back of her house. It may not have seemed like much to them, but they had accomplished about what I expected.

I followed Samantha back to Sussex. My first stop was at Marilyn's Café. It was nice to walk in and be recognized. People like to go where everyone knows your name. I gave Marilyn a big hug and told her I was looking forward to dinner. Marilyn's cooking was worth the drive.

Samantha had gone ahead to Gabe's office. Gabe was very interested in our findings in Washington. Samantha filled had him in on all the details and Gabe had come to the same conclusions I had: It didn't appear that we would be able to locate all the veterans on our list.

While we were in Washington, Gabe had exhausted his sources looking for several of the last remaining men. He had scoured numerous websites. The G.A.R. site was coming up empty of information. Local historical societies and museums were fruitless as well. The scope of the extended research that was needed was far beyond our realm.

We talked for about an hour. I wanted to drive over to Vevay and visit Dorothy and Gene. I called first to make sure they would be at home. Dorothy was pleased to hear my voice. Gene was resting, but she was certain that he would be up to some company.

As I was driving along the Ohio River, I remembered my first trip here over two years ago. It had been so exciting to be starting a project like this. It seemed like yesterday.

Dorothy met me at the door. She is a grand lady. Gene was walking with a cane across the living room as I came into the house. The stroke had affected his left leg but he was in good spirits. Gene asked me right off the bat, "Have you talked to that Butler woman?"

"Yes, Gene, I have. I have some very important things to talk to you about. Miss Butler met with Marilyn and I back in January. She truly felt horrible about your stroke and blamed herself. I think that because of your stroke, she came to some conclusions on her own that will have very positive results for us."

I went on about the meeting with Krista. Dorothy sat in on the conversation. Gene was dismayed by Krista's revelations. I told him I was going to Kentucky next week to follow up on Krista's advice.

Gene commented that he had heard some scuttlebutt about Civil War soldiers when he was a kid. He hadn't mentioned it before because he thought it was old nonsense. "You know how it is, rumors and things like that. Heck, I was only eight, maybe nine, years old. There were several old-timers around back in those days. We thought nothing of it then. I sure wish I'd sat down and talked to one of them."

"Gene, what exactly did you hear back then?"

"Oh, I don't know. I know some of those guys were very old. I think one of them was around 110 or so. I saw him in a parade one summer. They made a big deal about him. Forgot his name. I think he was from this area though."

"He probably was, Gene. There were hundreds of men from Vevay and Madison alone. Over in Springbrook Cemetery in Madison they have over 300 graves. Maybe your old soldier is there, resting in the sun."

"I suppose he is. I just remembered all that since my stroke; isn't that weird? All of a sudden like. I was telling Dot that I can still picture her on our wedding day. The other night we were watching T.V. and I told her to put the boys to bed because it was getting late. I sometimes think my mind is playing tricks with me."

I looked at Gene and smiled. He was ill and he may be right. I doubted that he would be able to return to work. He enjoyed it so but our research demands a sharp mind and an even better memory. I would miss talking to him on the phone. His voice always resonated with excitement. Dorothy sat next to Gene on the sofa, patting his hand. She knew.

I had every confidence that my conversation with Dorothy and Gene would go no further. They were old school—a secret was a secret.

We visited for about two hours. Dorothy was taking good care of Gene. I promised to visit again and to bring Marilyn the next time. I told Gene I would keep him posted on our progress. I gave him a hug and thanked him for all his work. Dorothy walked me to the door. Tears welled up in her eyes as I gave her a kiss on the cheek. I wiped away the tears and assured her I would be back.

I can't say I'd ever miss the drive from Vevay to Sussex on Route 129. That road is a winding narrow, nightmare. I have never found anything that compares to it. It's twenty-one miles of pure excitement. I can't imagine driving that road in the dark, or after having a few at a party!

I phoned Marilyn at her aunt's house and told her I would be spending the night is Sussex at the Four Seasons Inn. Harry, the manager, was still there. After checking in, I called Samantha's apartment. Gabe answered the phone. They were waiting for my call. While I drove into town, they walked to Marilyn's. I was ready for some down home cooking.

At dinner I listened to a wrap-up of what Gabe and Samantha had been up too. They had searched what we thought were the best places to find information. Samantha had tried to recoup information from pension files to no avail. Gabe had done likewise with discharge records at both the local and national level. The Internet system was growing fast. More and more data was being loading into the system. I knew it would only be a matter of time before the information we needed would be available. It could happen at any time. Our project was not going to last much longer. Everyone sensed the end coming. Aside from Deanna and Marilyn's discovery of Frederick Gale, our well had run dry.

After dinner we walked to Samantha's apartment. I wanted to talk to Gabe alone. Gabe suggested that he and I walk to the liquor store. Samantha thought nothing of it. As we walked the three blocks, I hinted to Gabe that there might be one last find in our research. I quickly brought him up to speed on Krista, I summarized Krista's letter and its possible meaning. Gabe immediately commented that there had been some resistance from various county officials that Samantha had contacted. Now he knew why.

I asked Gabe if he knew of a connection between any of the soldiers he originally wrote about and Wingo, Kentucky. He couldn't recall any such connection. He didn't believe any of the men from Kentucky who came north to enlist had come from that part of the state. It seemed to be too far away.

I shared all I dared with Gabe. I would save the rest for when we completed the project. I wanted to play out all possible leads before we called it quits.

After a brisk walk in the cool, summer air, and some lively conversation at Samantha's, it was time to get to bed. I drove to the Four Seasons. Tomorrow I'd head back to Sycamore. Marilyn would be home in a couple of days and I needed to mow the lawn before she got there. Marilyn took such wonderful care of the yard. She'd appreciate my help.

Chapter 12

*"You see things and say, "why not?" But I dream things that
never were and say, "why not?"*

George Bernard Shaw

On Saturday morning I called Wes around 9:00. He had been
up since 6:30 working on a cedar chest for a niece's birthday
gift. He said he had some coffee and for me to come on over.

Wes only lived a few blocks from my house. I was there in
a matter of minutes. I could hear the hum of the planer
even before I got out of my car. As I entered his workshop,
the sound was almost deafening. Wes had on earplugs and
safety goggles. He had become so used to the noise that it
was second nature to him.

Upon seeing me, He turned off the planer and the motor
wound down in a steady drop of decibels. "Coffee, Mike?"
Wes asked.

"Sure, that's why I'm here."

"Really? How do you like it, with or without sawdust?"

"Without if possible. I wanted to update you on our research
and what we've found so far. You know about most of it
already. But I have some new information too."

"Great, let's hear it."

"Well, Marilyn and Deanna located where Frederick Gale is buried. He was a businessman in Effingham but he's buried in a potter's grave. Seems he lost everything after the stock market crashed."

Wes poured our coffee and then wiped off a couple of old chairs he had in the shop. "Have a seat."

"Wes, I have another trip to take for the project. I was wondering if you wanted to come along since you're the one that got me in this thing?"

"When are you planning on going?"

"I can go whenever."

"I'd love to go. I have to finish this chest by Thursday. I can go next Friday or so. Where are we going anyway?"

"Kentucky, Wingo, Kentucky. Ever hear of it?"

"No, can't say that I have."

"It's in the Paducah area. We can drive there in about nine hours or so. I'd like to look around and follow a lead I have. We might be gone for two, three days."

"No problem. I have nothing planned for the weekend. It'll be a mini vacation. Mary won't mind."

"Good, I just wanted to run that by you and see if you were interested. I'm looking forward to it."

We visited for another hour or so and then I went to the university to finish up rearranging the office. Dr. Darling had moved Jim Brackett into our area. Deanna had had to give up a little space, but his addition to the research team was worth it. I was almost looking forward to the day when I could use Jim's services to help in my work. I hadn't done much in the way of medical research, but at least now we had an expert in the department.

As I opened the door to the research lab, I saw Joanne Darling standing in the middle of the room. She and Jim had started without me and were planning the floor design. We moved this desk here and that desk there. The file cabinets were a bit more difficult. We had four desk units in all to arrange: mine, Deanna's, Jim's, and David's. I suggested we set them up similar to what I had seen on T.V. police programs: in pairs, facing each other, in the middle of the room. I thought it would save space. At first Joanne wasn't hot on the idea. Jim liked it. One thing I hate in an office is when everything is slammed against the outer walls.

After setting up the desks in an agreeable arrangement, Jim and David began running the cables for the computers to each desk. Each of us would now have our own phones and a desktop computer. We had come a long way over the years.

I told Joanne that I was leaving for Kentucky on Friday morning. Whenever I was out of the office she tended to oversee things.

Jim said he'd be in the office most of the weekend. Deanna was off to see friends. David Hinman would be in and out.

Wes was packed and ready to go when I pulled up in front of his house. He was excited about being part of the team. We had a long drive ahead of us. Wes knows how important coffee is to me. He brought the largest thermos I have ever seen.

We talked about everything under the sun. I rambled on about all the things we had managed to come up with during our research. Wes was not an academic, but he had a fairly good understanding of history. I explained to him the dilemma I was in over the Arlington headstones. Parts of the puzzle just didn't fit.

We had a good time together reminiscing about the past and the various things the four of us, Mary, Marilyn, Wes, and I had done. We had camped together, taken day trips together, spent several weekends at bed and breakfasts together; we have shared more than twenty New Year's Eves together. We had our own history.

I stopped at a gas station in Paducah, just off the interstate. I asked the clerk for directions to Wingo. He said I had about a thirty-five-mile drive. I took his advice and followed Route 45 southwest toward Mayfield.

Upon reaching Mayfield, Wes suggested we stop and have dinner. I was game, of course. We looked for some place that might represent the area's cuisine. I had a hankering for some real southern fried chicken. We found just the right establishment outside Mayfield.

I asked our waitress if she could recommend a motel in the Wingo area. She said there was a small motel about halfway between Mayfield and Wingo on Route 45 called The Southern Belle.

It was about 7:45 when I turned off Route 45 and into the archway of the motel. I noticed only five, maybe six, cars in the lot. The motel was an old, L-shaped structure, probably built in the 1960s.

We both went into the motel office. There was no one at the front desk. I rang a small bell that sat on the counter. From behind a bifold door immerged a woman whom I suspected to be the front-desk clerk. I later discovered that her name was Melissa and she was the motel owner.

Melissa cut quite a picture. She was a brunette with big hair. I mean, she was right in the swing of things with fashion. What I remember most about Melissa was her attire. She wore an elastic collared, boat-neck white blouse that left her shoulders bare. Her shorts were what I think are commonly called "Daisy Duke" style. She had a small tumbler that always seemed half-full of bourbon. Melissa was memorable.

After checking us in, Melissa asked, "What brings you Illinois boys to Wingo?"

I fielded the question. "We're doing a little research in the area and we need to talk to someone in town."

"Oh yeah, who are ya' here to see? I know everyone in these parts."

"A lady named Judy North. Do you know her?"

"Of course I know Judy. She's a waitress at the Mill Café in town. Does she know you're coming to see her?"

"She's a waitress?"

"Yeah."

"Well, no, she doesn't know we're here at all. I was told I could find her almost any day in Wingo."

"That part's right. She works damn near every day. She only takes off when the place is closed. It's the only decent place in town to eat. Most folks head to Mayfield or Paducah for a real meal out. By the way, what do ya' need to talk to Judy about that needs ya' drivin' all the way down here?"

"Oh, nothing of interest really. Just a few questions, that's all."

"Must be something real important for you to come all this way. The Mill opens a 5:00 for breakfast. Folks down here don't sleep too late."

Wes and I awoke about 7:00. We drove into Wingo and parked across the street from the cafe. There must have been a dozen pickup trucks lined up in front of the Mill. We walked in and took a small table in the center of the room. It was obvious that we were from somewhere else. The locals eyed us up and down.

As I was looking down at the menu, a tall, thin, blonde waitress approached the table. She appeared to me to be in her late forties. She introduced herself. "Good morning, I'm

Judy, and I'll be your waitress this morning. Can I get you some coffee while you look things over?"

So this was Miss North. Krista didn't tell me anything about her. She only thought that Judy had information that I might find helpful. I felt pretty stupid at this point. It had been a long drive to Wingo and I was beginning to think that Krista was having a good laugh at my expense.

When Judy came back to the table with our coffee, I asked her if she knew a Krista Butler. Her composure turned somber. She stopped in her tracks.

"Yes sir, I know her. Are you the man from Illinois?"

"I am Dr. Carls, yes."

"I'm pleased to meet you. I told Miss Butler that I would help you with something. I can't talk to you right now. Let me get your breakfast and then I'll be back."

We ordered breakfast and took inventory of the environment in the restaurant. The people seemed friendly enough, but there was an aloofness about the place. Neither Wes nor I felt comfortable. I personally had the impression that I was being watched.

Judy brought our bill to the table. As she picked up our plates, she hinted for me to look at the bill. Under the guest check was a small note. It read:

> *Meet me in front of the library at 4:30. I will talk to you then. I will be in a green Ford Mustang..*

I looked at Wes. We were both surprised. We weren't thinking anything like this. She sounded so mysterious.

Wes and I had a lot of time to kill between now and 4:30. We decided to acquaint ourselves with the area. We had originally planned to return to Mayfield and see some of the historical sites. I knew that there were several Confederate monuments in the area. This entire part of Kentucky had been fiercely local to the southern cause. Before driving to Mayfield, I suggested we look around Wingo.

Wingo was a small community: old buildings telling of busier days gone by, small shops, a farm implement dealer, and a used car and truck lot. The streets were narrow, some paved, some not. There were no sidewalks in the residential area. The sign on the edge of town claimed the population to be 560. I guessed there to be about 125 homes in the immediate town area. A good description would have to include the terms rural and farming. There wasn't much of a business district.

Wes and I drove around the residential area and out into the countryside. This part of Kentucky was made up of vast rolling, wooded hills. There were many unnamed dirt side roads. I was certain a wrong turn would find us lost.

I had a map of the area so we drove to the even smaller hamlet of Water Valley, an old Confederate camp, Camp Beauregard, located just outside of town. Back in 1862 the camp housed an estimated 5,000 troops. The buildup in force was done to protect the area from Union troops based in Paducah. There never was an attack.

We found this region rich in Civil War history. For Wes and I, it was sensational. We thoroughly enjoyed the dirt roads and the monuments. One could easily visualize Union and Confederate troops moving amongst the trees and over the rolling hills. Fascinating!

We had to be careful about following directions. The main road was one thing, but those back roads were something else. Again, it was easy to get lost, maybe permanently in these backwoods.

We turned off the highway just outside Mayfield. I believe the name of the road was Pritcher Road. I followed this road into Mayfield proper, the county seat of Graves County. The monument in front of the courthouse was legendary because it had a drinking fountain built into it. At any rate, it was worth seeing. We also took a look at the famed Confederate Gates at Maplewood Cemetery. Wes was especially enjoying this free time. I enjoyed it as well, but I kept thinking about what information Judy might have for us later. Why was she so secretive?

We ate a late lunch at a small diner in Mayfield. It was around 3:35 when we headed back towards Wingo. In relation to Mayfield, Wingo is like taking a step back in time.

I parked in front of our motel-room door while Wes went in to get his camera. As I waited, I caught a glimpse of Melissa walking out of the motel office. She was walking towards me. I had the air conditioning on in the car. Melissa put both hands on the side of the car and bent over to look at me. I put down my window.

"Little hot for you Yankees down here?"

"A bit," I replied.

"What you boys been up to today. I hear ya' took a drive."

"Who told you that?"

"Small town; can't do nothing around here and not be noticed."

"I see. Well, we just took in some of the local highlights, you know?"

"Well, I'll tell ya' what, why don't you and your partner come on down to my office later. I'm cooking some salt pork and greens. I've got plenty. Plus, maybe I can answer a few questions for you about some of these local yokels. They don't bother me much anymore, but I can sure tell you some dandy stories if you're interested."

"We just might take you up on that. I enjoy a little gossip now and then. You can plan on us being there. What time are you serving?"

"Oh, I don't know, how about 7:00?"

"Okay then, we'll see you later."

Melissa turned slowly and walked back to the office. She made quite an effort to make sure I watched every step she took. I looked at Wes. He just smiled and then turned the air up a little higher!

Wes and I arrived at the library shortly before 4:30. It was only a matter of minutes before Judy arrived. As Wes and I got out of our car Judy pointed to a picnic table off to the side of the library. We followed her lead.

The temperature was climbing. There was no breeze and the air seemed stale. Judy came right to the point. "So, how much do you know about Project Unit Blue?"

I must have looked totally shocked. Judy continued, "Oh come on, Krista told me about you and your project. We haven't got a lot of time here. Please, let's get to the point. You have been on a roll with your research. The whole system is going to burst at the seams in just a matter of months. Krista felt that you deserve to know the entire story and that's why you're here, right?"

"But why here?"

"Dr. Carls, I have been with the project for eleven years. I know that must come as a real shock to you. I have been authorized to bring you up to speed. Let's start with the original project."

"Sure, but do we want to do that here, at a picnic table?"

"Fine, let's go over to my house. Do you have anything going tonight or do I have your undivided attention?"

"Wes and I told the lady at the motel we'd have dinner with her, but that isn't until 7:00."

"You mean Melissa? Be careful of her. She's the town gossip. No one really knows her story. Her husband up and left her a few years ago. As you probably noticed, she likes the bottle. She talks too much too. Watch what you say around her."

"No problem. Can we go and talk before dinner?"

"Of course. Follow me. I live over on South Street, about four blocks from here."

With that, Wes and I followed Judy as she led the way. I was so excited. Wes was trying to figure all this out in his head. I told him what little I already knew about Project Union Blue from Krista's note.

About a block or so from Judy's house, a county sheriff's car turned in front of me from a side street. The car came to a stop. Wes and I sat there wondering what we might have done wrong. I couldn't think of a thing. I knew I wasn't speeding and hadn't run a stop sign.

The officer exited his car and walked back toward me. I rolled down my window. The officer introduced himself as Officer Jeffrey Wade and asked for my driver's license.

"Did I do something wrong, Officer?" I asked.

"Nope, just checkin' things out here. You boys from Illinois?"

"Yes sir."

"Just wonderin' what you're doing here in Wingo. I hear you've been here a day or two."

"Yes, we're staying at the motel on the edge of town."

"What business you got here?"

"We're researchers, sir. We're leaving Sunday morning."

"Well, we just take notice of strangers in the area, that's all. You fellas go about your research and don't cause no trouble here. Got it?"

"Yes sir. I got it."

As Officer Wade walked to his car, I turned and looked at Wes.

"What the hell was that all about?"

"Man, I don't know, but it sure was strange."

I parked in front of Judy's house. She was standing in the driveway waiting for us.

"I saw ole' Wade pull you over. What did he have to say?"

"Strangest damned thing that ever happened to me. He wanted to know what we were doing in town. Does he stop everyone that passes through here?"

"No, he's just very protective of our little town. You know the type, big fish in a little pond."

"Gotcha."

"Anyway, don't worry about him. He'll be hanging around watching you the rest of the weekend. When did you tell him you're leaving town?"

"I said Sunday morning."

"Be sure you do. He'll be watching. Enough about that. Project Union Blue: This whole thing started back around 1945. Everyone knew that the last Civil War veterans were dying out. It was only a matter of time before they would all be gone. As I'm sure you know, the last Union reunion was in 1949 in Indianapolis and the last Confederate reunion was two years later in Norfolk, Virginia.

"To make a long story short, let me put it this way. There were people in high places who didn't want the South to have the last veteran. So, even before the NSC was founded, a plan was hatched to save some of these old soldiers. If you look at the facts, there were twelve known Union veterans in 1949. Only six attended the reunion. Why? The answer is simple gentleman: Project Union Blue had the others hidden away."

I sat there in awe. Wes was still reeling from the information I gave him earlier.

"Judy," I asked, "you're not telling me that the government was playing a game with these guy's lives, are you?"

"Yes, Dr. Carls, that's exactly what I'm telling you. As far as the original planners, and later the NSC were concerned, these six old men had no families and no real future. It was just a matter of keeping them alive to outlive their counterparts in gray."

"Wow, that's incredible." I couldn't even respond intelligently.
I could hardly comprehend a scenario like the one Judy had described.

Finally, I asked Judy, "So why are you here?"

"I'm here to introduce you to my daughter McKinzie."

"Your daughter?"

"Yes, she's a nurse. She lives in Mayfield. You're going to meet her tomorrow."

"But what does she have to do with this?"

"She has some very interesting information for you concerning Union Blue. You two enjoy your dinner with Miss Melissa and remember, don't mention any of this. My advice to you is to sleep in in the morning. I'll be at the Mill working. Come in for breakfast around 9:00. I'll give you directions to McKinzie's house. Old Wade will be watching you, so be sure to let him see you leave town. He'll be satisfied. Now go to your dinner."

"But Judy, I have so many questions, you can't leave us hanging."

"I'm sure you have thousands of questions. In good time, Dr. Carls, in good time."

Wes and I left Judy waving from her front porch. I drove straight to the motel. It was 5:35. Sure enough, Officer Wade was parked just down the street from the motel, just close enough to keep an eye on us.

Wes got out of the car first and walked slowly towards the door to our room. As I opened my door, Officer Wade pulled his squad car up behind me.

"Y'all have a nice dinner now with Miss Melissa. Have a good night."

I didn't respond as the squad car rolled away quietly.

Wes was watching from the window. He opened the door and asked, "What did he have to say?"

"Oh nothing, he was just letting us know he's keeping an eye on us, that's all."

"Man, they sure don't like strangers around her, do they?"

"I think it's more than that, Wes. There has to be more."

Melissa stood outside the motel office and waved to Wes and me. "Soups on, get it while it's hot!"

We walked down to the office and entered Melissa's private living area. Actually, we walked through it to a patio out back. I was surprised to see about a dozen other people there. I recognized two as other motel guests. I had no idea who the others were.

Melissa had cooked a whole hog. It was wonderful. The aroma filled the night air. There was a large oval shaped watering tank filled with ice and beer. Party lights were hanging off the eaves and in the trees. The music was upbeat and perfect for a warm southern spring night.

I asked, "Melissa, what's the occasion?"

"Nothing special. I love doing this. Once the weather gets warm enough, I have a party for my guests and a few friends every Saturday night. Don't you like it?"

"Oh, I think it's great. Thank you."

"No problem, just have a good time."

We ate and had a couple of beers as we talked to the other motel guests and Melissa's friends. After a while, I had the opportunity to talk to Melissa alone.

"So why are you alone in a small backwoods town like this?"

"Ya' know, everyone asks me that. Truth is, I like it here. People are real. They live simple little lives, but you know what, they know how to live. They enjoy life. No stress, no crap."

"I can see you like it. But how did you get here?"

Melissa's mood changed somewhat. She became more serious.

"I came here with my husband, Jim, five years ago. He was in construction and there was plenty of work on the interstate. About three and a half years ago he got killed on that road. Some damn drunk hit him in a work zone. Killed him outright.

Damn fool was going ninety miles an hour. Poor Jim. We had just bought this place and planned to retire here someday. Now I just stay here. Jim's buried over in Mayfield. I get over there from time to time. I suppose you've noticed I live in this bottle? For a girl from New York, life has sure dealt me a strange hand."

"Melissa, I'm sorry about your husband. Have you tried to sell the motel and maybe move back by your family?"

"No. I've learned to like it here. I like the pace. I can visit Jim every so often and life's not too bad. It gets lonely, sure, but then I have friends."

"So what do you think of Judy North?"

"She's great. When Jim and I first came here, she was involved in something. Never did figure that one out. Then, all of a sudden, about three years ago her daughter moved back here and Judy started working at the Mill. I think her daughter lived in D.C. or some place out east. She got divorced and moved back here by her mom. I hear she's a nurse at the medical center in Mayfield. Don't see much of her here in Wingo."

"You don't know much about Judy though?"

"Like I said, it all seemed kinda secret. These little towns around here all have secrets. I found out the old lady out on Brown Road was once the mayor of Lodi Springs. She was also a hooker in Chicago twenty years ago. They tried to keep the lid on that one for years. It eventually got out. I hear all kinds of crap."

"But you can't find out anything about what Judy used to do?"

"Believe me, I've tried. They're pretty tight-lipped about whatever it was."

"Interesting. So she just showed up one day from nowhere?"

"I guess so. You can't tell me that a woman like her has been a waitress all her life. Nothing wrong with waitressing, but I just think she has a past."

"I agree. She does seem to have a lot on the ball."

It was fairly obvious that Melissa didn't know anything about Judy or her past. She didn't pry for information either.

Wes and I stayed at the party until midnight. We told Melissa we had to be up and on our way back to Illinois early in the morning and that we'd had an enjoyable evening. Melissa had a real sense of southern hospitality.

Wes and I arrived at the Mill Café just before 9:00. The early morning breakfast crowd had come and gone. There were only six other customers having coffee or breakfast. Judy acknowledged us and said she'd be right over to take our order.

"Good morning gentlemen, what can I get you today?"

Wes and I each had coffee and a house special breakfast platter. In Wingo that meant eggs, grits, bacon, sausage links, and toast . . . truly a regional flair.

Shortly after we began eating, Officer Wade came through the front door. He walked across the restaurant and glanced at the two of us, then sat at the counter. Judy brought him a cup of coffee, decaf, with two creams. He was a regular.

As Judy turned to attend to other customers, the officer grabbed her wrist. Judy turned abruptly. I saw Wade whisper something to Judy. The expression on her face became a look of shock. Something was wrong. Perhaps something had happened to her daughter
McKinzie.

Almost immediately Officer Wade approached our table. Wes spoke up, saying that we were leaving Wingo as soon as we were done eating. Uninvited and to our surprise, Wade pulled up a chair and joined us.

"You boys won't be going to Mayfield today. It's been arranged for you to meet Judy's daughter McKinzie elsewhere."

"How did you know we were going to meet her?"

"It'll all be explained to you later. Just finish your breakfast and meet me out front when you're done."

The officer stood up and walking directly out the door without another word. I signaled for Judy to come to our table.

"Judy, what was that all about? How did Wade know about us meeting McKinzie? What did he tell you?"

"I want you two to just do as he said. I'll be with you in just a few minutes. Things are happening very fast. I'll buy your breakfast. Just do as Wade said."

Judy made her rounds to the other customers with coffee refills, clearing the plates. Wes and I finished our breakfast and sat for a few minutes trying to make sense of this whole situation. We had no idea what Judy meant by things were happening so fast. What things? Yesterday Judy had warned us about Wade, and today she appeared to be part of something with him.

Cautiously, Wes and I walked out of the restaurant. We didn't know what to expect. Officer Wade was standing next to my car and as I approached the driver's side he smiled and offered a handshake.

"Dr. Carls, I hope I didn't alarm you too much. You have nothing to fear. You're not in any trouble. I want you and Mr. Wilson here to follow me. Judy North will be accompanying us. She'll be along in just a minute."

"What is this all about?"

"It's about your research, Doc. It's what you've been looking for all along. Judy will fill you in. Just follow along."

Wes and I got in my car and waited. Judy came out of the Mill and went straight to the squad car. Judy had a big grin on her face as she waved at us and motioned for us to follow Officer Wade.

We followed Wade heading southeast. The road went from blacktop to gravel as we drove for nearly eighteen miles through forest and marsh areas. We passed a large lake with stagnate water. The morning fog was still hanging over the lake. The water was covered with dust and algae. Small gnats and water bugs hovered above the mist. The backwoods road was winding and becoming narrower. We were in what I found out later to be a national forest.

Suddenly, Wade stopped his car in the middle of the road. It didn't matter since there were no other vehicles around. As he walked back to my side of the car, I was a bit fearful. I didn't know what to expect out here on a backwoods road, alone, and in a strange area.

I rolled down my window. Wade bent over and assured me everything was okay.

"Just up the road here a piece is a gravel lane on the right. I want you to follow that road for about a hundred yards and park your car. Then I want you to walk up the hill another hundred feet or so and you'll see a small white house off to your left. There'll be a young man there named Case looking for you. McKinzie Lovell will be there, too."

Wade walked back to his car and drove slowly ahead. It wasn't but a half mile or so and I could see the narrow drive on the right. Wade pulled up just beyond the drive and stopped. I turned right just behind the squad car and followed the lane.

The forest was very thick and dark. Tall trees blocked out most of the sunlight. It was deafeningly quiet. The gravel crunched under the tires of the car. I did as Wade had instructed, and parked. Wes and I exited the car. The forest was cool for this time of day.

As we walked, only the chirping of the crickets and an occasional cawing of crows broke the silence. I recognized the kudzu vines by their distinctive hairy leaves and racemes of purple flowers. Our footsteps became rhythmic on the loose gravel.

After a short walk, Wes pointed to the left. "There's the house."

To get to the house, we had to step over a two-foot wide drainage ditch that followed the road. The water was an inch or two deep and crystal clear as it trickled down the hillside. I noticed a swirl in the water where small tadpoles were swimming amongst the rocks.

Beyond the small white house was a green-and-white mobile home with two vehicles parked nearby. A navy blue Ford sedan was next to the house and a dark green pickup truck was parked by the mobile home.

As Wes and I approached the house, a young man opened the screen door. He looked to be in his mid-twenties. He was casually dressed in jeans and a long-sleeved flannel shirt.

"Dr. Carls and Mr. Wilson?" he asked.

"Yes."

"Good morning, we're expecting you."

Wes and I exchanged handshakes with the young man.

"You must be Mr. Case. Officer Wade said you'd be here."

"Yes sir, Special Agent Derek Case, FBI."

"FBI?"

"Yes sir, stationed here since last July."

Just then a young lady in a nurses uniform entered the porch from the main house.

"Hi, gentlemen, I'm McKinzie Lovell. I believe you've met my mother, Judy?"

"Yes, ma'am, we have."

"Well, come on in. I have been authorized to bring you up to speed with Project Union Blue."

McKinzie led us into the small house. As we entered there was a small but well-equipped kitchen to my immediate left. The living room area took up most of the house. There were two overstuffed sofas and a leather recliner. On the far wall was a bookcase next to a T.V. on a stand. I noticed two smaller T.V. screens next to one of the sofas. The room was inviting and pleasant.

To the left, halfway between the kitchen and the far wall, there was a door leading to an adjacent room. The door was closed.

McKinzie asked us to sit as she continued to explain.

"Gentlemen, your project has been under the close eye of the NSC. Krista Butler has monitored your every move. We all knew that someday, someone would stumble onto Project Union Blue. You have come very close. The NSC has been involved in this project since its inception.

"I have the honor and privilege today to fully explain the project to you. I will also be introducing you to Private Jacob Winslow."

My heart was pounding in my chest. Impossible! How could that be? A Civil War soldier still alive? Impossible! McKinzie hardly reacted to the shock on Wes's face and mine.

"I know, this must come as a real shock. Jacob has been with Union Blue since 1951. The NSC found him in an old-soldiers home in Indiana. I believe you're familiar with that part of Indiana, Dr. Carls?"

"Yes. What town was he living in?" Somehow the words came out in the correct order.

"In Vernon."

"Really?"

"He had been living there for nearly forty years. The people there never located any family for Jacob. That is where you come in, Dr. Carls. You have found family members for some of these men. Just like James Blocker. We actually had two of our project members come from that home in Vernon."

"Two?"

"Yes, Jacob, and Thomas Caldwell. Mr. Caldwell passed away in 1971. Jacob took Thomas's death very hard. Now Jacob is the last one. Would you like to meet him?"

Wes answered first. "Yes. Is he here?"

"Yes, Mr. Wilson, just inside that door. I'll have to ask you both to put on a sanitary suit and mask."

McKinzie and Agent Case helped Wes and I into the blue plastic suits. Each suit had a small breathing apparatus on the back. We wore matching blue latex gloves as well. Wes was extremely excited. This was a moment in time. My thoughts were swirling in my head. *Was this real? Was it really happening?*

McKinzie had also suited up. Although we had on full head covers with clear facial shields, we could still hear each other clearly. McKinzie asked Agent Case to open the door.

We quickly entered the room, which was larger than I expected. In the center of the room was a glass-enclosed room within a room. A blue fluorescent light hung over the hospital bed. The glow of the light cast an eerie scene but the soft background music was comforting.

I looked closer. There was a glass door on the opposite side of the room. McKinzie told me to go to the door. I did as she said and stopped.

In the bed lay an old man. What little hair he had was the purest white I have ever seen. His skin appeared chalky in color. There were large brown age spots on his face, particularly under his eyes, which were deep set and barely open. The skin on his arms and hands was nearly transparent. There was an IV in the back of his right hand. His blue veins protruded from his skeleton-like hands. He was wearing an oxygen nosepiece and behind his head was a breathing pump and other monitoring equipment. He appeared to be comfortable and relaxed.

McKinzie let reality set in. Wes and I were both nearly brought to tears. This was truly a profound moment for us. We were doing our best to control our emotions. It wasn't easy.

I asked McKinzie, "How old is he?"

"Jacob was born on September 29, 1848. He's 140 years old."

"My God."

Wes asked, "Can he speak?"

"Oh yes, he also responds to light and noises. We talk to him all the time. Would you like to talk to him?"

This was out of our league. Wes and I looked at each other. The opportunity to talk to a man 140 years old had its own responsibilities. What would be an appropriate question? I could only imagine the things in history he must have witnessed. It was overwhelming.

"Dr. Carls, would you do us the honor? I'd like you to go in and whisper the names of Jacob's colleagues in his ear. I want to see how he responds. Can you do that?"

"Of course. It would be an honor."

I slowly opened the glass door and entered the room. The temperature in the room was quite warm and I began to sweat in my suit. I could hear Jacob's breathing. I moved toward the ancient man and approached him cautiously. Jacob rolled his head towards me and opened his deep blue eyes wider. Jacob realized I was a stranger. The beeping on the monitor became louder. McKinzie motioned for me to touch Jacob's hand and I slowly placed my right hand on his left wrist. The beeping slowed down a pace or two as Jacob calmed down.

I leaned over and put my face about two inches from his ear. In a low whisper, I began saying the names I had come to memorize from the list of missing soldiers of the 14th Indiana.

"Thomas Bean . . . James Bannon . . . Ben Alt . . . Charles Dix."

I paused and swallowed. Jacob's response so far was minimal.

I continued, "Frederick Gale . . . Robert Ackley . . . Hiram Oaks . . . Horace Tidall . . . Thomas Caldwell."

Jabob's heart rate markedly increased. His reaction was obvious. He recognized Caldwell's name. I stopped whispering the names. McKinzie nodded to me. She had the response she was looking for. I stood there looking at this unique man. He turned his head and followed my movements. I looked at Wes. It was his turn to come into the room.

I started to turn about to walk to the door when Jacob gave my hand a gentle squeeze. I stopped. Jacob's lips were moving, but I heard no sound. I leaned my ear close to his lips. Then the most amazing thing happened. In a voice that was as clear as could be, but as soft a whisper as could be imagined, Jacob spoke.

"Winslow, my name is Winslow."

I was so choked up that I couldn't speak. I patted his hand and nodded my head with tears in my eyes. Jacob stared at my face. I looked into those blue eyes.

"I know who you are. I know you're Winslow."

My breathing was rapid. I was overcome with sadness for this last warrior. He seemed at peace. He had lived so long. If he saw the world today he would feel so out of place. Slowly I laid his hand on the bed beside his hip. Jacob watched my every move as I walked to the door.

McKinzie met me at the door.

"Isn't he amazing?"

I hugged her. How could I thank her for allowing me to be here?

Wes entered the room and stood at the foot of the bed. Jacob, watching as Wes moved to the far side of the bed, slowly brought his hand to his chin and made a pulling motion. Wes laughed out loud. Jacob was figuratively recognizing Wes's beard. Wes smiled in agreement and did a likewise motion. Jacob blinked his eyes and turned his attention to the far wall in the room. Wes and I both followed his stare.

There, on the wall, was a picture of a group of Civil War soldiers. With his hand, Jacob pointed. McKinzie walked with me around the glass room and took down the picture. She had an idea. Perhaps Jacob could identify the men in the picture.

"Oh my God," she said, "he knows these soldiers. Let's try something. The picture can't go in the room. I'll hold it next to the glass. Dr. Carls, you go back in there with Mr. Wilson. I'll point to each soldier one at a time. You say their names slowly. Maybe Jacob can give us some kind of indication if he recognizes anyone."

I eagerly joined Wes. It was worth a try. McKinzie pointed to a man sitting in the foreground. I began reciting the names of the men in the 14th Indiana once again.

"Robert Ackley . . . Ben Alt . . . James Bannon . . .Thomas Bean."

As soon as I said Thomas Bean, the monitor began to beep. Jacob raised his hand ever so slightly. McKinzie moved her finger to another soldier standing next to a tree.

I continued reciting the names . . ."Jacob Bendalone . . . James Blocker."

Again, Jacob reacted.

Again, McKinzie moved to another soldier.

"William Bergman . . .Thomas Caldwell . . .Charles Carr . . . Elijah Childers . . .Charles Dix."

I stopped. Jacob closed his eyes. McKinzie put the picture down and came around the glass room. "That's enough for today. Jacob has to rest. Mr. Carls, you have permission to come back for another visit. Let's go into the other room and talk."

Wes and I agreed and left the room. In the living room we disrobed the sanitary suits. I looked at the small T.V. screens by the sofa and saw Jacob resting in his bed.

McKinzie offered us a seat.

Agent Case offered Wes and I a beverage. While he was in the kitchen preparing the drinks, the door from the porch opened.

A short, dark-haired lady in a navy blue blazer and matching skirt entered the room. McKinzie stood and made the introductions.

"Mr. Wilson and Dr. Carls, I would like you to meet Special Agent In Charge, Lori Fuller. Lori has been with Jacob for nine years. She has been well briefed on your research."

Agent Fuller was quite talkative. "I take it you've already met Jacob?"

I answered, "Yes, we have."

"Great. Isn't he wonderful? I have been in Nashville for a couple of days. Derek and I rotate shifts watching Jacob. Miss Lovell checks in every other day or so and is always on call. I would imagine you have several questions for us right about now?"

"McKinzie," Wes began, "have there been many visitors to see Jacob?"

"Mr. Wilson, I'll let Agent Fuller answer that for you."

Agent Fuller stood in the middle of the room and addressed Wes's question.

"Jacob has had many visitors over the years. At first, from 1951 until 1960 or so, no, it was a secret assignment in the agency. However, once the last certified Confederate veteran, Walter Williams, died in December of 1959, the story started getting out. People at that time would have looked at the project in a different light. The NSC determined to keep Jacob in safe houses, where he would be protected.

"As far as other visitors, yes, there have been doctors from Johns Hopkins, the World Health Organization, the Centers for Disease Control, and the United Nations. He has also been visited by every president since Harry Truman. President Reagan was here last October."

"And no one found out about these visits?" I interjected.

"That's right. I can't say who, but we brought one president here riding in an eighteen-wheeler. Jacob likes visitors. If you ask him, he'll proudly point out his medals."

McKinzie turned in her seat and pointed to a display case on the opposite wall. I looked at the case. Wes was the medal expert here.

Wes walked over to the case. "There are three purple hearts, a Lincoln Campaign medal, three I don't recognize, and believe it or not, a Medal of Honor."

"Yes," said Agent Case, "President Kennedy presented it personally to Jacob in 1962. Jacob was living in Silver Springs, Maryland, at that time."

"How many times has Jacob been moved?" I asked.

Lori Fuller answered. "Over the years the NSC has moved Jacob whenever anyone got too close to exposing the project."

"And now?" Wes added.

"Now, it's all coming to an end very soon. For all projects the NSC has to comply with the new laws on freedom of information within the next six to eight months. This will all come out. You should also know that Jacob's health is failing much more rapidly than the doctors had expected. There isn't much more we can do for him. He has been so strong for so many years. There will be no more moves for Jacob."

Wes and I sat there taking in all that the agent had said.

Finally I asked, "How do you think the public is going to respond to a government agency keeping a human alive as a medical experiment?"

"Dr. Carls, the NSC has just completed a nationwide survey addressing that very question. From what I have been told, the results are very favorable for the agency."

"I have one more question, Agent Fuller. How is it that the local people in Wingo and the surrounding area don't know about you guys out here?"

"Well, sir, we're very careful with our cover. McKinzie lives in Mayfield and works at the medical center. She drives here using a private road on the opposite side of the national forest from the road you came in on. Agent Case lives here full time but does venture out on occasion. I probably come and go more often than anyone. I usually enter and exit the grounds at night under the cover of darkness. You can probably guess that we don't shop or eat in the local towns. That's been the lifestyle for all the agents that have served in Project Union Blue since day one. The local law enforcement agencies have sometimes been made aware of our presence. Officer Wade has been in his job for nearly thirty years. He's a professional and can be trusted. He knows this part of the country like the back of his hand and keeps people away. He was brought into the fold shortly after Jacob was moved here."

"Where was Jacob living before the move here?" I asked.

"He lived in a very rural area of Virginia, in Willis, Virginia. The agency moved him here in secret because, like yourself, some researchers were getting close to finding him."

McKinzie stood and suggested that Wes and I take one last look at Jacob on the monitors. She hinted that it was time for us to leave. She went on to explain that if we wanted to visit again, there were channels open to us. She gave me a phone number where she could be reached.

"One more thing before you go," McKinzie said. "Krista had an agent deliver this envelope for you, Mr. Wilson."

Wes took the manila envelope and opened it. He read the contents to himself first. Wes looked at me and then at McKinzie before he spoke.

"Wow, they found Thomas Overland. Krista says that he was a fireman in Chicago after leaving Indiana in 1880. He retired in 1903 and died in 1921 at the age of 82. She says she had two NSC employees dig through census records. Overland is buried in St. Mark's Cemetery in Lisle, Illinois."

Wes gave McKinzie a warm handshake and told her to thank Krista.

Agent Case escorted Wes and I out of the house and back to our car. He instructed us to drive forward through the forest and exit on Purchase Highway. It was a long three-mile drive through the dark woods.

Wes and I had just experienced the most incredible event in our lives. We turned onto Purchase Highway and didn't stop driving until we reached Paducah.

I called Marilyn at home. It was a lazy Sunday morning for her. She slept until 10:00. I told her that we were getting a late start and probably wouldn't get in until after 10:00 tonight.

Wes and I talked about Jacob all the way home. For now we knew we couldn't share what we had seen. I was only in that room with Jacob for ten minutes, but it was the most amazing ten minutes of my life. Wes felt the same way.

We talked about the other soldiers that were in the program along with Jacob. We didn't get any information on them. Who exactly were they? When did they pass away? Did they have families? We wanted to know. I would call Krista and ask these questions.

Chapter 13

"The more sand that has escaped from the hourglass of our life, the clearer we should see through it."

Jean Paul

It was certainly good to be home. In reality, Wes and I were only gone for a little over forty-eight hours. The difference between Wingo and Sycamore could be measured in light-years!

Marilyn and I stayed up and talked most of the night. It was an incredible story. I could hardly wait to get to the university and share what I could with Deanna.

I arrived at the research lab around 7:30. No one was there yet. I knew Deanna would be coming in soon. Realizing the time difference, I decided to call Gabe and Samantha. I thought for sure that at least one of them would be in the office.

The phone rang several times. I was just about to hang up when a hurried Samantha answered. She had run down the stairs to get the phone.

"Dr. Carls," Samantha said with a winded voice, "how are you? We hadn't heard from you. Gabe thought for sure you'd call from Kentucky. How did things go?"

I was bursting to tell her. "Oh, Samantha, you won't believe what I found in Wingo. I only want to tell the story once. Is Gabe going to be in soon?"

"Yes, he should be here in a matter of minutes. What is it?"

"No, no, I want to talk to both of you at the same time. You can set up a conference call, right?"

"Yes, I can do that. Is it that important?"

"It couldn't be more important. You set up the call when Gabe gets in. I'll be here in the office all day. Our phone system is equipped for up to a six-way call. I'll tie in Deanna as well. Please call just as soon as Gabe gets in. Okay?"

"Sure, Dr. Carls, just as soon as he gets in."

"Alright, I'll talk to you in just a few minutes. Bye for now."

"Bye, Dr. Carls."

I felt like a little kid with the best secret in town.

Deanna came in the door and tossed her book bag on her desk. She looked at me like there was something wrong.

"So, Boss, how was your weekend? Mine really sucked!"

"Mine was great, Deanna. What happened to you?"

"Oh, let's just say I screwed up big-time in the personal life department."

"Should I ask with whom?"

"Go right ahead and ask. It's probably a thing of the past by now anyway."

"Did you and David have a falling-out?"

"David Hinman? Are you crazy? Dr. Carls, for a smart man you sure miss a lot that goes on around here. No, not David. How about Jim Brackett?"

"You and Jim?"

"And what's wrong with that?"

"Nothing, I guess I never put two and two together."

"Well, we did. Anyway, like I said, it's probably all over with. Me and my stupid mouth. I guess I thought it was more serious than he did. Anyway, how was your weekend in Kentucky?"

"I'll tell you all about it when Samantha calls back. I want all of you on a conference call so I can tell everyone at the same time."

"Don't tell me we lost our grant."

"No, Deanna, nothing like that."

"Are you and Jim going to be able to work together, assuming this thing is really over?"

"I think so. I can't believe you didn't know about us. Right here under your nose."

"I guess if you're not looking for it, you don't see it."

"True, how very true."

The door to the lab opened slowly and Jim Brackett came in. He gave me a slight wave and then walked to Deanna's desk. With the new office layout, that was quite easy to do—they faced each other!

Jim put his arm around Deanna's shoulder and kissed her on the cheek. Deanna turned to him and I could see that she had started to cry. I thought it best to excuse myself for a few minutes.

"Um, Deanna, I think I'll grab a coffee at the vending machine. We're expecting that call from Samantha. I'll be back in a couple of minutes. Just grab the call, okay?"

Jim looked at me and said, "Sure, Doc."

When I came back, Jim was sitting next to Deanna at her desk. Deanna was much more composed. She was actually smiling and laughing.

"Well, the sun appears to be coming out," I said.

I never was good in emotional situations. These two obviously had something going on between them. Now that I looked, it was all so obvious. They were in love.

While we were waiting for Samantha's call, I had a question or two for Jim.

"Jim, what's the longest a human has every lived? Do you have any idea?"

"Sure, as a matter of fact there was just an article in *JAMA* about that very topic. Let me get the magazine. I know I have it here somewhere."

Jim went to his desk and searched through a stack of magazines and papers. He pulled out two copies of the *Journal of the American Medical Association* and thumbed through them.

"Here it is, a Japanese man named Izumi. He died in 1986 at the age of 120. The article says that there have been other reported cases in the Soviet Union that people lived to be 140 or older. The Soviet cases are undocumented since they had no birth records. In 1947, the Soviets said they had a woman who claimed to be 156 years old. Incredible, huh?"

"But this Japanese man, they have documentation?"

"Yes, that's what it says. He was born in 1865."

"How would you treat someone that age?"

"I suppose a regulated diet; do body checks, watching for lumps or moles; look for bruising. We can do so many things now. If a person's organs are working, I guess you just take safety precautions and make sure they don't fall and break something. The doctor's would surely monitor blood pressure and maybe do bi-monthly blood work or something along those lines. Check with the staff at a nursing home. They do daily exercise programs and such, but usually unless the person is sick, they should be okay."

Jim added, "You know, Doc, we are living longer. We have more people over the age of one hundred than ever before. It must be all that fast-food we eat nowadays!"

I was just about to ask Jim another question when the phone rang. It was Samantha and Gabe. I told Deanna and Jim to set their phones on conference call even though they were only ten feet away. I wanted them to share in Gabe and Samantha's reaction to my news.

Gabe asked, "So how was the weekend? You must have something thing pretty good the talk about to warrant a conference call."

"Good morning, Gabe. Yes, I do have something pretty good to talk about. I want to make sure that I have everyone's attention. This is really important. Wes and I had a great time in Wingo. We met Judy North, just like Krista Butler arranged. We met several interesting characters in Wingo. Anyway, we met Judy's daughter, McKinzie Lovell. McKinzie is a nurse. I have to back up here a bit.

"Back in January, Marilyn and I met Krista Butler in Chicago for dinner. At that time, Krista told Marilyn and I about a project called Union Blue. The project started in the late forties, even before the NSC was founded. At any rate, the project is still operating. The purpose of the project was to keep Union veterans alive as long as possible. There was a real sense of jealousy because the last Union and Confederate veterans were dying out very quickly. Like I said, the project is still operating."

There was silence on the phone. I think everyone knew what I was going to say, but they wanted to hear it.

I continued, "Wes and I had the opportunity to meet a living Union veteran."

At that point, I heard a unified gasp. Everyone, including Jim Brackett, was shocked by my statement. I could sense that they had a hundred questions.

I said, "I know, that sounds impossible. Believe me, it's not. We met and talked with Jacob Winslow. He's 140 years old."

I stopped.

"Dr.Carls," Samantha stuttered, ". . .that's . . .that's unbelievable . . .impossible."

I asked Gabe, "Well Gabe, what do you think of your research now? Was it worth it?"

Gabe was speechless. Finally he said, "I never dreamed anything like this. I can't believe it. Is it really true?"

"Yes, Gabe, it is. And you know what, I am taking you to see Jacob for yourself just as soon as you can arrange it. We have a standing invitation. I have permission to take each of you down to see him. His health is okay for now, but failing. The NSC people have to expose the project very soon under federal law. They gave me a list of all the veterans that were in the project. At one time back in the fifties, they had five men in Project Union Blue. Jacob is the last. I know you all have questions for me. Let me talk to Gabe for now and then, Gabe, you can share with Samantha. Is that alright?"

"Yes, Mike, that's fine," said Gabe.

Deanna, Samantha, and Jim hung up their phones. I continued telling Gabe more details of Union Blue and the other soldiers that are buried in Arlington. Deanna and Jim overheard my half of our conversation. Deanna was now in tears. All our work, the countless hours of researching, visiting county courthouses, digging through old records, finally over.

Over the next five months I made the trip to Wingo four times. I took Gabe and Marilyn on the first trip. We stayed in Mayfield and entered to forest on the private back road. We did not go into Wingo.

On the second trip, Deanna and Jim accompanied me. I should also mention that they were engaged by this time.
Being a medical researcher, Jim was most anxious to see Jacob and talk to his caretakers. Deanna and McKinzie formed an instant bond. They are so much alike . . . bubbly and outgoing. We had a tremendous time.

Dr. Darling asked if she could possibly visit with Jacob. I made the appropriate call and received permission for Joanne's visit. However, I could not get away at the same time as Joanne. Krista Butler agreed to come to Illinois and meet Joanne at Moss and drive her to Wingo. I knew that Krista would be able to answer any questions Joanne might have. They had a good visit with Jacob.

In June, Krista called me and told me that Jacob's health had taken a turn for the worse. Samantha had not had a chance to get to Wingo so I called and made arrangements so she and Gabe could make the trip.

The news of the NSC project was about to break. I wanted to see Jacob one more time. Marilyn and I drove to Wingo over the Fourth of July weekend. We met Judy and Krista at the Mill Café Officer Wade was there, still keeping a close eye on things. I introduced Marilyn to Officer Wade. He could be quite a gentleman with the ladies.

As Marilyn and I arrived at the little white house, there seemed to be an air of sadness. McKinzie met us at the door. I thought. for sure that Jacob must have passed away. McKinzie asked Marilyn and I to have a seat in the living room. I looked at the monitors. Jacob was resting just fine.

McKinzie satdown next to Marilyn. Taking her hand as she looked at me, she said, "I just received a phone call from Deanna. I'm sorry to be the one to have to tell you that there has been an accident. David Hinman was killed last night in a car accident in Chicago. Deanna just found out this morning. I'm so sorry."

Marilyn and I knew David well. He lived alone and had been a dinner guest many times. Marilyn was very fond of him.

Marilyn asked McKinzie if she knew if any arrangements had been made.

"I don't think so. Why don't you call Deanna and find out?"

Marilyn made the call. Deanna was still understandably upset. She said that Joanne Darling was taking it very hard. David had been her right-hand man for two years and they had had a great working relationship. They respected each other so much. All far a arrangements thought, none had been made. David's parents had passed away several years ago. Deanna knew that he had a sister who lived in Washington state. To Deanna's knowledge, no one had contacted her yet.

Marilyn told Deanna that we would cut our visit short and be home Sunday afternoon. I fully agreed.

The five of us, Marilyn, Judy, Krista, McKinzie, and I all visited with Jacob that Saturday afternoon. He was alert and smiled often. Marilyn held his hand most of the time.

It was during this visit that Jacob was the most talkative. At one point, while we were talking and perhaps ignoring Jacob, he pulled Marilyn's hand and wanted her to look at him. His lips began to move. Marilyn leaned closer to hear. Jacob, in a very clear voice, said, "I wore a blue coat." Then he smiled at Marilyn. Marilyn kissed the old soldier on the forehead.

"And I bet all the girls thought you were quite handsome in that coat."

Jacob actually chuckled. He was so animated that day. We even tried to identify a few more men in the picture. Jacob's vitals were very weak. We couldn't say for sure if he recognized anyone. It was an honor just to be there with him. He was history alive.

I was alone with Jacob for a while Saturday night. I did know if he understood me or not, but I told him how we had located many of the men he fought with. I said some of their names again for him. I mentioned towns and battles and various things that were part of his past. As I walked around the bed in the glass room, Jacob's eyes followed me. He would roll his heads from side to side. McKinzie let me feed him dinner that night.

Marilyn and I had both done this on our previous visit, but this time it seemed special.

At 9 o'clock it was time to leave and return to our motel. We had a long drive the next morning. Marilyn was in the living room. I motioned in the video camera for her to suit up. She understood. As I left Jacob that night, I, too, kissed his forehead. He slid his hand up toward my elbow and gently pulled me toward him. I hugged Jacob for the first time. He tried to wrap his arms around me. His eyes were watering. He didn't want me to go.

I walked out of the little glass room and turned to look at Jacob. He followed my moved. I stood at attention and saluted the old soldier. Jacob attempted to do likewise. It was a very special moment for each of us.

Marilyn came in the room as I left and I watched her on the monitor. She went directly into Jacob's little world. She took his hand as she sat on the side of the bed. Marilyn held his hand as she rubbed it with the other. McKinzie looked at me and said, "Jacob really likes Marilyn. He doesn't usually show that kind of affection. Look at them together."

Marilyn stayed with Jacob for about ten minutes. She slowly placed his hands on his chest. Then she leaned over and kissed him on the cheek. Jacob reached up slowly with his right hand and placed it on Marilyn's left cheek and whispered a solitary word, "Love." He and Marilyn were both crying.

241

Marilyn wiped his tears away with the bed sheet, then rose from the bed, wiped her own tears, and walked out of the room. Before she left the outer room, she blew a kiss through the glass. Jacob waved good-bye very slowly. As his hand came to rest on his chest, he closed his eyes.

As Jacob slept, Marilyn and I visited for another hour or so with Krista and Judy. McKinzie had gone home to Mayfield. Krista told Marilyn about all the years of joy and frustration with Jacob and the other veterans that had been in the project. Then she revealed the best news of all.

"I should tell you that because of the avenues you have opened up with your research, we believe we have located Jacob's family. The agencies involved, the IRS, the census bureau, and the military, are all fairly certain that we can pinpoint relatives in Cincinnati."

"That's wonderful," said Marilyn.

"Yes, it is. Unfortunately, the powers that be don't think it's a good idea to have them come here to see Jacob. I don't quite understand their reasoning, but at this point, it isn't going to happen."

I jumped in, "My God, why not? I would think the family would want to see him. Think of how proud they'd be."

"I agree," said Krista, "but it's out of my hands. As a matter of fact, it's out of the NSC's hands too."

"So, has the family been contacted?" Marilyn inquired.

"I don't think so, yet."

I glanced at the monitor. I couldn't help but think how long it had been since Jacob knew any family. It must have been so lonely for him. He looked at rest.

Marilyn and I left the house and drove to our motel in Mayfield. We planned on waking early and getting back to Sycamore to deal with a much much more solemn task.

We didn't realize it then, but I think we might have sensed it. That would be the last time we'd see Jacob.

♣ ♣ ♣ ♣ ♣ ♣ ♣ ♣ ♣ ♣ ♣ ♣

Chapter 14

"They say that all good things must end someday, autumn leaves must fall . . ."

Song Lyrics
Chad & Jeremy
"Summer Song"

David's funeral took place on Wednesday, July 6. It was the type of day that David would have enjoyed: beautiful clear sky, in the upper 80s, with a gentle breeze.

David's sister, Nancy, and her husband, Bob, had made the trip from Seattle. She said she hadn't seen David since he came to Moss. The funeral was well attended by the faculty and staff of the university.

Nancy made arrangements with Deanna to go through David's personal items at his office. Joanne Darling would be there as well. Nancy and Bob were staying at Joanne's home. I told Nancy that David had been such a help to me with our research project. He was the one who located the G.A.R. website that proved to be so helpful.

After the luncheon, Marilyn and I went home to relax. It had been a very hectic six days. Marilyn had planned dinner at our house later that evening for Nancy, Bob, and all our research staff but we had several hours to ourselves in the afternoon.

The phone rang just as Marilyn was bringing me an ice tea on the deck. It was Deanna. Krista Butler had left a message at the office apologizing for NSC. They had planned on sending flowers for David's visitation and funeral but somehow the person in charge of making the call to a local florist failed to get it done in time. I had already planned on calling Krista on Thursday as a routine follow-up to our visit to Wingo.

On Thursday, Krista and I had a most informative conversation about the entire Union Blue project. We discussed the men buried at Arlington in Section 244. I found out from her that four of the five had lived into the late 1960s. I knew that Caldwell died in 1971 and that Jacob was the last to remain.

Krista seemed relieved that the project was being made public. It made her job much easier. Krista mentioned that she may be moving into a new area for the NSC, stem cell research. I had heard of it, but it was not only a highly complicated science, but one that incorporated moral concerns as well. Krista ended our conversation by saying that she would keep in touch and let me know if there was any change with Jacob.

The last month of summer seemed to slip by. August was especially hot. I had originally planned another trip to see Jacob, but it didn't work out.

On September 17, Krista called me at my office and said that there had been some changes in the staff in Wingo. Lori Fuller had been transferred back to Washington and Derek Case was also due to transfer soon. McKinzie would still be there, but a new security detail would be in place. Krista also reported that the following Friday would be her last day on the Union Blue project. She reaffirmed the fact that I still had an open invitation to visit Jacob. In conclusion, Krista said very remorsefully that Jacob's health was continuing to decline.

I wished Krista well on her new assignment. We had gotten off to a bad start, but that was all behind us now. She was actually a very caring person.

The national press was made aware of Project Union Blue during the last week in September. Surprisingly, the public reaction was very supportive. Of course the southern newspapers claimed it was a fraud. Prior to Winslow, the official last Civil War soldier was Walter Williams who had died in 1959 in Houston, Texas.

I was interviewed by three different Chicago television stations, but beyond that, nothing. Several national publications ran articles and some pictures, but no big splash.

I believe the NSC was just as baffled as I was. There was no haggling about scandals or cover-ups. There was no call by the moral majority for investigations into "God playing."

I called Krista at the NSC as soon as the news broke. It was good to hear her voice. She seemed less stressed. She said the people in Washington had braced for a flood of attacks over the project, but they never developed. Her new work was going well. I told her that I still wanted to get back to Wingo, but that Joanne Darling had been keeping me busy. I would try to make the trip in October.

Two weeks after talking to Krista, Marilyn and I received the call we knew and feared would come. Jacob Winslow had passed away in his sleep during the night. McKinzie was in tears as she told Marilyn how Jacob had recognized Marilyn's picture and how he had gestured, putting his finger on her face. It was all happening so fast. McKinzie said that Krista had been notified and that the NSC was handling all the arrangements.

The funeral was to take place at Arlington National Cemetery and would be a national event. Of course Marilyn, Deanna,

Gabe, Samantha, and I would be attending. Krista Butler called and asked if Marilyn and I could arrive a couple of days before the funeral. Krista had made arrangements with the NSC to have Jacob's family attend a reception in their honor.

Krista knew without asking what my answer would be.

Marilyn and I arrived at the Sheridan Hotel shortly before noon the next day. The reception for Jacob's family was scheduled at 7:00 that evening at the Smithsonian Institute. I called Krista to let her know we were in town.

The reception was a very formal event. I met several officials from the NSC and other federal agencies. I wondered to myself, *How many other secret projects must these people have up their sleeves?* Krista was there by herself. She took Marilyn and I to the head of the receiving line and introduced us to Jacob's great-great-granddaughter, Beverly, her husband, Charles Gates, and their son, John Jacob. They were living in Cincinnati. Krista explained to the family that it was only through our efforts that the NSC had been able to locate them after all these years.

I chatted with Beverly for some time. She told me how her great-grandmother had talked about her great-great-grandfather Jacob and how he had gone to war. They had lived in Switzerland County, Indiana, and were married there. She thought that the reason we couldn't find any information on him was because Jacob had taken his wife's last name in order to avoid his father's bad financial record. Then Beverly scolded, "If we had known about Jacob years ago, we could have told someone all this."

I explained to her that there are many misleading things in Civil War records. Many times researchers have to rely on family bibles and folklore. Marilyn told Beverly what a wonderful man Jacob was. Beverly, of course, had never had the opportunity to meet him.

The pitch of Pastor Brigham's voice brought me back to what was happening. I once again focused on young John's face. He never took his eyes off me. I heard Pastor Brigham end his prayer with a resounding Amen! I must have been day dreaming.

The vice president stepped to the podium. His voice was soft, barely audible. The microphone volume needed to be adjusted. I thought his words were textbook in nature, not very personal. His words were lacking emotion for such an occasion. Although near the end of his eulogy, the vice president made a startling comparison. As he commented on the four members of Project Union Blue that preceded Jacob in death, he referred to them as accounted for. In referring to Jacob, he counted him as present. As a final offering, the vice president announced the promotion of Jacob Winslow to the rank of general. This had become tradition for the last surviving soldier in American conflicts. The large crowd was silent. Respectful. The honor guard, erect at attention, stood at "Present Arms."

The pallbearers lined the caisson on both sides. They grasped the casket with their white-gloved hands. Slowly, they turned.

The honor guard commander gave the order, "Attention!"

The crowd stood in silence. The military drummers beat a low, muffled cadence. The pallbearers walked in step, slowly, to the gravesite.

The casket, draped in full military honors with a thirty-three star flag, was placed over its final resting place in Section 244. Finally, Jacob joined his fellow comrades.

Reverend Brigham stepped forward and offered a final prayer.

Two of the honor guard members stood at either end of the casket. In precision form, they raised the flag from the casket. Quietly, they made the traditional thirteen folds. The senior officer, a lieutenant, bowed before Beverly Gates. In a firm but humbling voice, he handed her the tri-fold flag and uttered those memorable words, "On behalf of the president of the United States and a grateful nation, we honor a fallen comrade."

The blue-clad honor guard brought their weapons to the ready. The order came: "Fire," a pause; "Fire," another pause; and finally, "Fire."

Immediately, the hallowed tones of a bugler echoed over the cemetery. Then there was a second bugle mimicking the first. Then a third. I have never heard "Taps" played so beautifully. There wasn't a dry eye in the crowd.

As the ceremony concluded, the vice president spoke to the crowd again and instructed the honor guard to fire one final salute. To my knowledge, this was the first and only time such a salute had been offered. All seven Civil War–vintage artillery pieces fired at once. The sound was deafening. Young John, standing in front of me, jumped.

Just as the crowd was settling down from the boom of the cannons, another roar came from the sky above as a squadron of F-14 fighter jets flew over in missing-man formation.

Marilyn, Gabe, Samantha, Deanna, and I made our way to Jacob's family. We hugged them and told them what an honor it was to be here and to have known Jacob.

I saw Krista in the crowd. She had been standing a short distance behind me with McKinzie Lovell. McKinzie greeted Marilyn and began crying out of control. I was told earlier that McKinzie was away on business with the medical center the night Jacob died. She missed so much and blamed herself.

"Poor Jacob, he was alone with people he didn't know. I should have been with him."

Marilyn tried to comfort her. McKinzie told Marilyn that it was the first time in five years that she hadn't been with him.

Marilyn simply said, "When it's your time, it's your time. There's nothing anyone can do about that."

"McKinzie sobbed, "I know, I know."

Our research team walked around the cemetery looking at the other gravesites in Section 244. The names on the headstones were familiar to all of us. I glanced beyond the tent and mound of flowers. There, lying on the ground waiting to be installed, was Jacob's headstone. The stone itself was an exact reproduction of the original government issue. It had a rounded top and an engraved badge on the front. The stone read:

Gen. Jacob Winslow

Co. G

14th Indiana Vol. Inf.

Slowly, we all said good-bye to Jacob and made our way to the gates of the cemetery and to our cars. The Smithsonian again hosted a luncheon reception for the four hundred in attendance.

Marilyn and I arrived back at the Sheridan shortly after 4:00. We made plans to meet Deanna, Samantha, and Gabe for a late dinner at 8:00 and I wanted to relax for a few hours beforehand.

At 7:45, Marilyn and I were standing in the lobby of the hotel waiting for the others to join us. A tall, slender man in a bellman's uniform told me that there was a call for me on the house phone near the elevators.

I followed the bellman as he led me to the phone and then walked away. I answered the phone.

"Hello."

"Dr. Carls, this is Judy North. I have to tell you something. Jacob is not dead. He's alive. They moved him. They moved him."

I was in disbelief. "What?"

"It's true, believe me, it's true."

I asked Judy, "Where are you?" The phone went dead.

I hurriedly went to the front desk and asked where the bellman had gone.

"Sir, we have no bellman on duty this evening."

"You have to have one. He just told me to take a phone call on the house phone by the elevator."

"No sir, those are public phones. Our bellman would never direct someone to those phones. Our lobby house phone is here on the counter."

Who was that man? I looked in panic, but never found him.

Marilyn could see that I was flustered. "What is it, Mike? What was that call about?"

I told her what Judy had said. It was unbelievable.

I used the house phone to try and reach Krista at work. No answer. I called information for her home phone. No listing.

Marilyn and I met the others at the restaurant. Jim Brackett had been at a conference, but he joined us this evening. My mood was saddened as I told everyone about the call. Somehow I knew it wasn't a hoax. Jacob alive! Where?

Our dinner was supposed to be a celebration. It was far from that. We discussed the funeral. What were the chances that the NSC would fake Jacob's death? We knew that they had been good at keeping secrets. Why not again?

Marilyn and I couldn't enjoy the evening. I just wanted to get back to the hotel and sleep. It had been a long day anyway, and now this. I couldn't contact Krista. I had no idea where McKinzie was staying in town, and Judy was . . somewhere.

I was sound asleep when the phone rang again. It was 3:00 a.m. I thought it might be Judy again.

"Hello, Judy?"

"No, Dr. Carls, it's Derek Case. Listen. Are you awake?"

"Yes. Yes."

"Tomorrow morning, go to the Ember Coffee House Café in Georgetown. There will be a man there who will contact you. His name is Gino Totter. Don't look for him. He'll come to you. He has to be careful. Be there at 10:30."

"Derek, can I trust him?"

"Yes, totally. He has some information for you."

"Do you know if Jacob is still alive?"

"Good night, Dr. Carls."

Marilyn asked, "Was that Judy?" She hadn't heard anything.

"No, it was Derek Case with the FBI. He said we have to be at a café in Georgetown tomorrow morning at 10:30. A Gino Totter will meet us with information. I asked him about Jacob, and he hung up. Bizarre."

I couldn't sleep another minute. I called room service. They were open. I asked for a pot of black coffee.

Then I called Gabe and Samantha's room. I explained what had happened. Samantha in turn called Jim and Deanna. The four of them came immediately to our room. We all had coffee and tried to assess what was going on. We decided to all be at the café.

Marilyn and I sat at a table in the café next to the front window. Deanna and Jim sat off to our left while Samantha and Gabe were across the room. Several other customers were seated throughout the room.

About ten minutes after sitting down, a tall heavy-set man with white hair and a full white beard approached our table.

"Good morning, Mrs. Carls, Dr. Carls. May I join you? My name is Gino Totter."

"Yes, Mr. Totter," Marilyn said.

I looked at the others. They were all focused on this man.

I happened to catch a glimpse of a black Toyota Camry parked directly outside the café. I looked closer. The driver appeared to be the same man who had worn the bellman uniform at the hotel.

At that moment, Marilyn leaned across the table and asked, "Mr. Totter, do you know anything about Project Union Blue?"

I turned my head to look at Mr. Totter. He was looking out the window at the driver of the Camry. I glanced again towards the car. The driver nodded his head at Mr. Totter as if a signal.

Then Totter answered Marilyn's question.

"Yes, I know about the project. There are several of us in the agency concerned about Jacob. I served on his detail some years ago. I know how the NSC hates to give up their secrets.

"I don't know exactly where Judy North is but she made a hurried call to Agent Case . . .

"Marilyn, did you know that the colors are beautiful in New England this time of year?"

My mind was racing, looking for answers.

I looked again out the window at the Camry. Realizing that Totter had relayed the message, the driver gave me a feint salute and slowly pulled away, disappearing around the corner.

♣ ♣ ♣ ♣ ♣ ♣ ♣ ♣ ♣ ♣ ♣ ♣ ♣ ♣

About the Author

Tom Oestreicher has been an avid Civil War enthusiast and collector for 35 years. Tom has taught history at both the high school and the collegiate levels. Oestreicher currently teaches at Genoa-Kingston High School and lives in Sycamore, Illinois, with his wife, Marilyn. Tom has two grown children and four grandchildren. In addition to Tom's teaching career, the Oestreicher's own and operate Tommy O's Family Restaurants in Sycamore.

Printed in the United States
23671LVS00005B/58-222